The Barefoot Farmer
The Best of the Barefoot Farmer

by
Jeff Poppen

Third Printing, 2002
Second Printing, 2001
First Printing, Barefoot Farmer Volumes I, II, III,
1996, 1997, 1998

The dates at the end of the articles signify when they were first published by the Macon County Chronicle, 1993-2000, although many have been substantially revised for this edition.

www.barefootfarmer.com

©Copyright 2001 Jeff Poppen "Barefoot Farmer", Red Boiling Springs, TN

ISBN: 0-9721378-0-7

printed on recycled paper

Acknowledgements:

Editing and Typesetting - Jim Durham, Coree White, Debbie White, Melissa Falls, Denise Rhoton, Mary Lou Ramsey, and Graci Quid
Book Design - Winthrop Brookhouse
Illustrations (from actual farm scenes) - Linda Johnson
Herbal Plates - Lenna Frances Keefer

I'm deeply indebted to my family, friends and neighbors for all their help and encouragement, and to the many others who have touched Long Hungry Creek Farm with their love, interest, and support throughout the last 25 years.

Foreword by Harvey C. Lisle

Not many young men know so definitely what they want to do in life as Jeff did after high school. His father, a retired college professor and avid organic gardener himself, offered to put Jeff through college, but Jeff had other ideas. He asked his father if he could take the money that would be spent on a college education and, instead, use it to help his brother buy a farm in north central Tennessee. It was far back in the hills with no ready access to electric power or telephone. It was almost like pioneer living. They eventually installed a solar power system which furnished light but not enough power for a refrigerator or other power consuming appliances. This was a good life which he shared with his partner, Debby Beaver.

I met Jeff when he and his father visited me many years ago. I was in biodynamic agriculture which was introduced to the world by Rudolph Steiner and deals with the spiritual side of agriculture. Not many people, including farmers, think much about the spiritual aspects of the land, the crops, the farm animals and the food they all furnish. The spiritual side of agriculture was of great interest to Jeff and he has pursued it vigorously. Although Jeff rarely writes directly on the spiritual side of agriculture, the reader can sense the reverence with which he deals with his subject. This reverence manifests in his organic and biodynamic approach to all aspects of his farming.

Well beyond his youthful years, Jeff, now with many seasons of organic and biodynamic farming, has taken on the role of teacher; maybe not a college professor but just as truly a teacher.

As you read the pages of this book you can picture yourself on a farm teeming with life. The farm, the experiences related to the farm and the food produced on the farm will all bring pleasures most people are not privileged to have. It is still true that it is the land which sustains us and Jeff deals with this subject beautifully.

CONTENTS

Chapter I: Elementals

The Importance
  of Organic Matter   3
Compost   5
The Metamorphosis
  of a Leaf   10
Soil Structure   13
Hauling in Manure   16
Cover Crops and Crop Rotation   18
Forces   22
Lime   24
Subsoiling   26
Manure Spreader   28
Marketing   30

Chapter II: Spring into Action

Seeds   37
Companion planting   39
Peas   41
Onions   44
Carrots   46
Parsley   48
Potatoes   50
Harrowing   53
Asparagus and Rhubarb   55
Wildflower Hike   57
Hoeing   59

Chapter III: Summer Bounty

Tomatoes   63
Peppers   66
Sweet Corn   68
Green Beans   71
Melons   73
Cucumbers   75
Butternuts   77
Sweet Potatoes   80
Hilling   83
Flowers   85
Weeds   87

Chapter IV: Autumn Arrives

Fall Garden   91
Chinese Cabbage   93
Garlic   96
Putting Foods By   98
Seed Saving   100
Chickpeas   103
Celery   105
Unusual Vegetables   107
Shiitakes   109
Goldenseal and Ginseng   111
Winter Covers   113

Chapter V: Berries and Fruit

Raspberries	119
Blueberries	121
Strawberries	123
Mulberries	125
Pears	127
Apples	129
Pruning	131
Grafting	133
Top Working	135
Persimmons	137
Wine	139
Cider	142

Chapter VI: Fields and Farmyard

Cows	147
Fencing	149
My New Love	151
Cheese	153
Hay	155
Corn	157
Wheat	161
Chickens	164
Bees	166
Orchard Mason Bees	169
Insects	171
The Food Web	173

Chapter VII: Cow Horns and Crystals

The Agriculture Course	179
Homeopathy	186
Cow Horns	188
Horsetail Tea	191
Barrel Compost	193
Death and Life	195
Elementals	198
Planting by the Signs	200
Thanksgiving	203

Chapter VIII: A Tennessee Homestead

Root Cellar	207
Work Days	210
Greenhouse	212
Cold Frames	214
Solar Electricity	216
Outhouse	218
Patio	220
Wood	222
Farm Tour and Dinner	224
T.V. Show	226
Biodynamic Conference	228
Vision	230

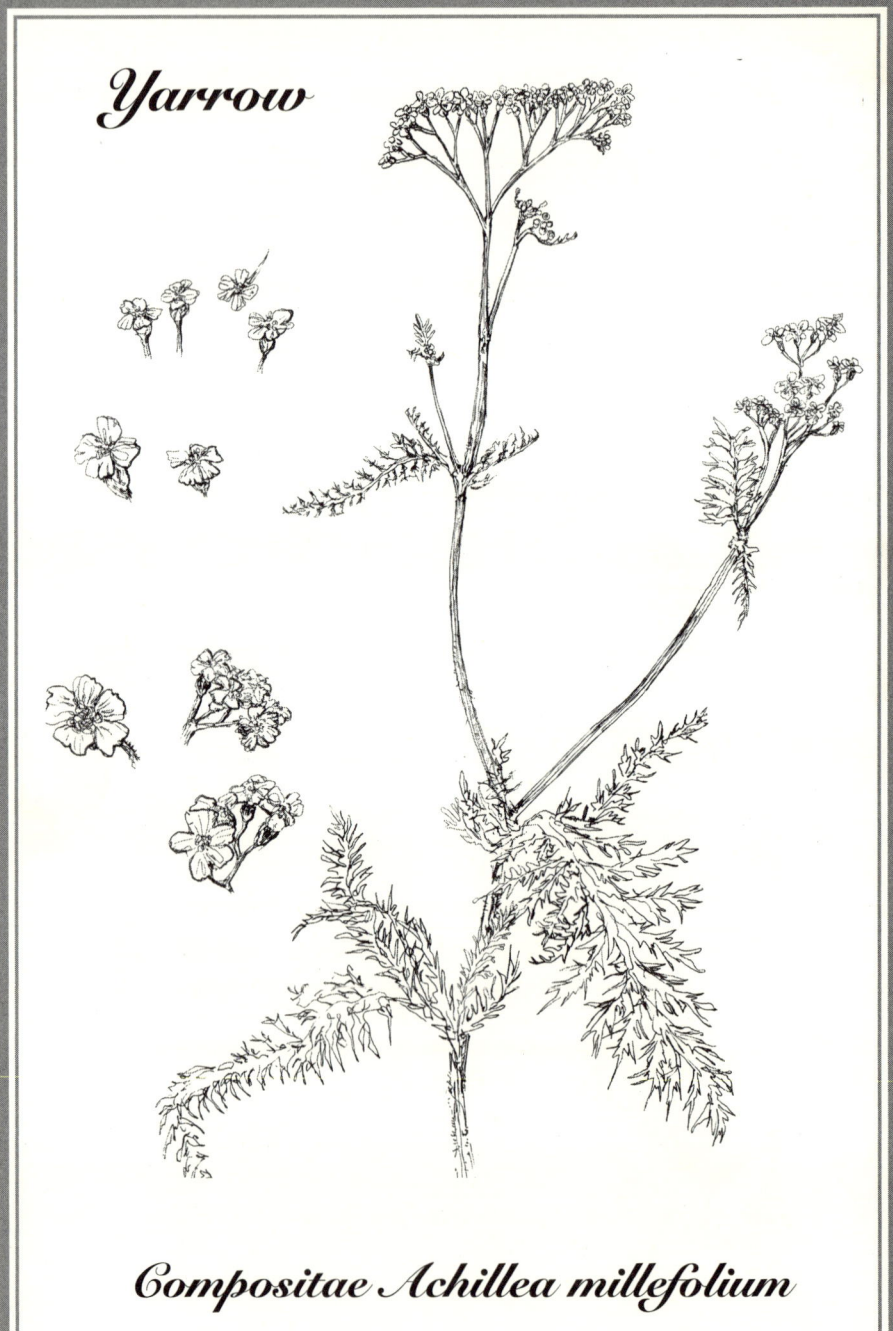

CHAPTER I

Elementals

The Importance of Organic Matter	3
Compost	5
The Metamorphosis of a Leaf	10
Soil Structure	13
Hauling in Manure	16
Cover Crops and Crop Rotation	18
Forces	22
Lime	24
Subsoiling	26
Manure Spreader	28
Marketing	30

"Agriculture . . . is our wisest pursuit, because it will in the end contribute most to real wealth, good morals and happiness."

Thomas Jefferson

The Importance of Organic Matter

The cornerstones to a healthy garden are biological activity and good soil structure.

Organic matter is necessary for all the little living things that make up the biological life in your garden's soil. The organic matter content of average soil is about 2%. It's the organic matter in soil that makes it dark and fluffy. Gardeners know that the darker and fluffier it is, the better the soil. Hard, cloddy soils have less organic matter, less bacteria, worms and tiny plants and fewer living and dying things altogether.

The natural process is that a plant or animal grows and dies, then decomposes to become plant food. This is biological activity. When the little living things in the soil die, their remains become available to the plants. As organic matter continues its decomposition, nutrients are released as available plant food. So a higher percentage, say 3% to 4%, of organic matter in your soil will mean more plant food. This is why it is so valuable to leave land in a cover crop or hay for a few years. The sod, as it grows and dies, helps to build up the organic matter.

Another way to build up the organic content of your soil is to haul it in. Manure, leaves, rotten sawdust, or other organic wastes can be mixed in your garden. The small living beings in your garden, from the tiny bacteria and microorganisms to the springtails and earthworms, all need air and water. The looser soils with more organic matter have more air and also a sponge-like capacity for holding moisture. My own experience indicates that air is the most important thing to get into my garden.

Luckily, the beginnings of biological activity are always present. Throw a banana peel out on the lawn and soon ants and bacteria will turn it back into the earth. Soils with a higher organic matter content have more biological activity and will digest the organic residue more readily, hence a quicker release of plant food and a happier soil life. Practically speaking, all gardens benefit greatly by adding compost, rotted manure, old leaf mold, black sawdust, rotted hay and other similar materials. By feeding our soil life we are indirectly giving our plants the best possible environment.

Chapter 1 Elementals

A symbiotic relationship is one in which two things are mutually beneficial to one another. In our humus-rich soils, you can pull up a plant and see a white, fuzzy web on the roots. I used to wonder if this was okay, but the plants seemed to be healthy so I didn't worry about it. Then, just a few years ago, I learned that this is a life form that allows plants to absorb soil minerals that are otherwise unavailable.

Good soil structure includes little air pockets, and we should try to retain the air pockets by carefully preparing our gardens in the spring with this in mind. Avoid using a rototiller. Granted, it makes the ground look fluffy after you use it, but it will pack up hard after the next thundershower unless you are quick to get a mulch on it or have unbelievably high organic matter. The constant rotating of the tines beats the soil into a fine seedbed at the expense of good soil structure. Rototilling masks the problem of soil structure temporarily while greatly aggravating it in the long run.

A disc can also be quite devastating to the soil's crumbly nature. I am still recovering from years of my over-discing. A gentle plowing with a mold board or a rebreaker, followed by a harrow and drag, is quite sufficient to get the ground ready to plant. Further tillage will happen as you cultivate anyway, so don't be so concerned with pulverizing the soil before you plant.

The old-timers around here know that the less you work your ground, the better your crop will grow. Another advantage of humus in your garden is that it forms carbonic acid with rainwater and will consequently dissolve some of the minerals from the parent rock material. By taking good care of our soil life, giving it air and rotten wastes, we create the foundation for healthy plant growth. Consequently, the food raised there will contribute to our own health.

May 24, 1994

Compost

What is the easiest way to create a rich humus and a garden full of life? Compost! The "organic" in organic agriculture refers to life, and by mixing organic materials with manures to make compost piles, we use life for our fertilizer.

In olden days, a huge manure pile was a sign of wealth. To impress a prospective bride's family, peasants were known to have borrowed a neighbor's compost pile just to have it near their place and appear wealthy. These peasants understood the value of manure, as their lives depended on it. By correctly composting it and returning it to their fields, they maintained a naturally fertile humus that allowed them to grow their crops.

A good garden soil is dark brown in color with a loose, crumbly texture and it's full of living beings. When these living beings die, their remains become the ideal plant food. It is this biological activity that has fertilized plants for eons and continues to do so in organic agriculture. All of the hungry beings quickly go to work on whatever falls to the ground, first turning it into their bodies, and then back into the soil when they excrete and die. The soil is like a big stomach, digesting whatever falls on it.

Who are these beings? We can see earthworms, literally farmers' and gardeners' best friends. Their castings and tunnels create wonderful soil. Pill bugs, springtails, centipedes, grubs and a host of other small insects inhabit a live soil, looking for food and eating each other. Above them are mice, birds, frogs, lizards and other creatures, also hungry and always eating and pooping.

Then there are all the small microorganisms, some living only a few moments before they die and become plant food. An acre of good topsoil may have 1,000 pounds of earthworms in it but could contain up to 2,000 pounds of protozoa and another 1,000 pounds of bacteria. With about one billion bacteria per gram of soil, these guys don't weigh much. A half a ton of them is a lot of mouths to feed; add to this all of the yeasts, fungi and algae and you have a hungry crew out there. What's for dinner? All of the plants and animals that die and start to rot. The greater the diversity and quantity of life in your garden, the healthier your plants will be.

The compost pile is the heart of the garden and fall is a great time to make one. There is plenty of garden refuse to gather and by spring planting time, you'll have the world's best fertilizer. Composting is rewarding and enlightening as we turn death into life. I prefer a shady spot for the compost pile so it doesn't dry out in the sun. It's handy to choose a place close to the garden. The ground should be well drained so the nutrients don't leach away.

A pickup truck loaded with manure, although not necessary, is a real boon to your composting operation. Manure is irreplaceable in many respects in farming and gardening. We have yet to fully understand the complexities of nature with regard to intestinal flora and microbiology. We do know that many living beings inhabit a cow's tummy. They live in the cow's four stomachs along with the cow's dinner, and special life energy is engendered there and then excreted. These live entities help things to decay and through their death create humus, which in turn promotes future life.

Many cattle farmers and horse owners will let you have a truckload of manure in return for cleaning their barn. Everybody gains when we clean barns and make compost. Manure is the nitrogen source for the compost and gets the pile warm and working. I'm a manure connoisseur, and although cow is my favorite, I like horse manure because it heats up, pig for root crops, and chicken for its high fertilizing power. I avoid manures from commercial confinement operations, because of all the chemicals they use.

Another element to consider is carbon, which grabs and keeps the nitrogen from fleeing into the air. Carbon is abundant in the garden, field or forest. First, I gather dry fibrous materials, like old corn-stalks, rotten hay and leaves, to make a bed for the pile. A foot and a half of loose carbonaceous material underneath the pile allows good access for the all-important air.

Next, shovel or fork the manure on, about three to four inches all over the pile. I like to start a pile about ten feet in diameter and build it up with sloping sides to about seven feet wide at the top. Round ones appeal to me, but if I have a large amount of compost material I'll put it into windrows eight feet wide and 20 or 30 feet long. After the manure, a sprinkling of good garden soil is a dandy way to ensure that the pile has the soil microorganisms present. They "teach" the manure and garden refuse how to rot; in other words, how to become soil. It's like adding yeast to your bread recipe. You can make bread without it, but better bread with it.

If you're pulling weeds for the pile, you have clumps of dirt with handles. Just bang them together and the micro-buddies fly all over the pile, happy to be in such rotten company. Pile on the old tomato vines, okra stalks, pigweeds and grass clumps. After a foot or so of this, layer on another few inches of manure and keep going. Other good things we add to our pile are rotten sawdust, kitchen scraps, pond muck and leaf mold. Anything that was once alive can be turned back into life-giving soil through composting.

Often it's a good idea to water the pile at this stage, especially if the manure is dry. We all know stuff rots when it's wet, so don't build a dry compost pile. Soak it down. You want it moist like a wrung-out sponge, though too much water will drown all your little helpers. A dry, white mold will appear on a pile that feels too dry to the touch, and it's a sign to add water. Keep on layering. By crisscrossing some big hollow ragweeds or cornstalks on the pile, you create air tunnels into the center of the pile. This will allow you to avoid the big job of turning your compost pile to get air inside. A well-built pile made in the fall will be ready by next May with no turning, but you can speed up the process by forking it over in a few months or poking holes in it with a large iron bar.

Rock dusts are another good thing to add to the compost pile. Soils in the South didn't get the last glacial activity and the resulting grinding up of rocks. Spreading rock dusts is a way to compensate for this because they help remineralize the land. Besides their specific mineral content, rocks have energy in them, which may be the reason that ancient cultures built rock circles and towers. Lime is the most commonly used agricultural rock dust, but is not added to a manure based compost heap because it dissipates the nitrogen. It is excellent to use in a plant-based pile, though.

We use colloidal or rock phosphate on our farm and in our compost piles. It is made by grinding up the rock called apatite that has a small, immediately available phosphorus content and a large reserve. Sulfuric acid is sometimes added to it to make superphosphate, which has much more readily available phosphate, but organic farmers don't use it. We want our plants to get their nutrients from a stable humus, not straight out of the bag.

Rock phosphate, also called pebble phosphate, is a mined product with a higher phosphate content. Colloidal phosphate is a by-product from the settling ponds at the mine, and has a finer texture. I use about 100 pounds per pile, or 600 pounds per acre if I am spreading directly. I believe composting helps the rock dusts go through an enlivening process. Granite meal is ground granite rock containing potassium and other minerals. We get ours from a Georgia quarry where it's a native rock and given away. Basalt is from Massachusetts, and clodbuster is from New Mexico. Greensand, a good potash source, is from old seabeds. All of these are valuable when sprinkled on the layers while making compost. I've also added flood plain debris and sand. When the pile is five feet tall, I leave a depression in the center of it to catch rainwater. A "skin" of hay or leaves will help shade it if it's in direct sun.

With the biodynamic method, which we've been practicing since 1986, small amounts of specially prepared plants are inserted into all the finished piles. I use a stick to make two-foot deep holes in the pile and put a little compost in my hand, then add a spoonful of the preparation to it, squeeze it together, and thrust it into the fresh pile. I use stinging nettle and oak bark in the center of the heap, and around the edges insert yarrow and chamomile on one side, dandelion and valerian on the other. (The article "Agriculture Course" has more information regarding the biodynamic preparations.)

The pile will warm up as it rots and then later cool back down; as the original materials lose their shape, earthworms and other small animals will appear. This "second stage" compost can be used on heavy feeders like corn or squash. At the third and final stage, it will be a dark brown, friable humus where nothing original is distinguishable, and can be used on vegetables, fruits, berries, flowers, herbs, pasture, lawns or anywhere you want to bring life energy into your land.

The place where the cows eat all winter is where we make our huge compost piles. They leave some of the hay uneaten with lots of manure around, so after they feed for a few weeks I scrape it up with a front-end loader, sprinkle in soil and maybe some rock dusts, and leave it to compost in a shady spot.

How much compost do you need? I spread one to two tons per acre for hay and pasture land and up to 20 tons per acre for crops, depending on what I'm growing. Even small amounts of compost have a wonderful effect on the soil life. In a garden bed, I toss a bushel or two every 100 square feet – more if the land is poor and less if the crop is not a heavy feeder.

Just give the invisible benefactors a chance and they will do their job. They've been doing it for eons, and all we need to do is quit poisoning them so they can get back to work. The effects will spread out over your garden and create a fertile haven for growing delicious food, and you'll have plenty of healthy weeds for next year's compost pile.

Compost happens!

March 28, 1995

Metamorphosis of the Leaf

The plant world astounds us with its diversity, but it is also quite interesting to look at its similarities. If we closely observe the annual flowering plants or the annual growth of perennials, we can see them as just one form - the ever-changing leaf. We can imagine the different parts of a plant as being the metamorphosis of a leaf.

It starts when moisture and warmth swell a seed in the ground, a root spirals downward, and a tiny shoot sprouts upward. The first leaves to appear don't necessarily look like the leaves that will develop later. They are often much simpler. For example, the crude first leaves of beans are often shaped similarly to the seed. These are followed by the first true leaves. Those first true leaves are still much simpler than what comes later.

As each leaf draws in air, it combines the air with its own moisture, and the plant stalk grows upward, the leaves spread out, and the roots grow deeper. The plant creates nutritive juices in ever-finer forms on its way to reproduction. More and more newly emerging leaves open up, looking like hands unfolding and holding an invisible ball. If too much soluble fertilizer is available at this stage, the plant will keep making leaves and flowering will be delayed. The leaves will keep trying to make finer juices, but too much nourishment will create cruder juices, requiring ever more leaves to deal with it. That's why if you over-fertilize your tomatoes, you get beautiful tomato leaves, but few tomatoes.

When the plant matures, a change happens. The leaves get smaller and narrower and the stem shoots up and the leaves all gather around in a cluster to form a flower bud. The flower bud (or calyx) is a contraction of small leaves, sometimes with a hint of the color to come. With excessive nourishment the plant would make more leaves; without it the plant feels the need to reproduce itself. The magic continues as the next transformation begins. The flower opens up, and lo and behold, the leaves have now become even finer and have turned into petals, glowing with colors other than green.

The next stage is another contraction into the organs of reproduction – the female, which is in the center as a continuation of the stem growth, and the male organs, which are the dangly things all around it. When fertilization takes place, often with the help of an insect, another expansion begins with the swelling of the fruit or pod. Both eventually dry up and contract. The last contraction is the seed, from which this whole beautiful process started. It's hard to see by just looking at a seed all the different forms it may grow into, but it's a helpful exercise for gardeners.

It is interesting to take all the leaves off a plant (preferably a weed, kids, not a garden plant) and arrange them in the order that they grew on the plant. That way you can see clearly how the simpler small ones at the base of the plant give way to gradually bigger leaves, reaching a point of perfectly representing that particular leaf. Then the leaves get finer and more pointed until they eventually wrap up the concealed flower. A similar metamorphosis can be observed by studying butterflies. First, the egg (the seed) lies dormant. Then it emerges as a small worm (the shoot stage), which gets bigger and bigger until it wraps itself in a cocoon (the flower bud), which will soon open into something altogether different, the butterfly (the flower), which eventually forms an egg again. You could say a butterfly is a freed flower, or a flower is a tethered butterfly.

The metamorphosis of a leaf was closely observed and written about by the German author, Goethe, who saw the whole universe as a living being. Modern scientific thinking works well in the inorganic-mechanical world, Goethe believed, but was inappropriate when applied to the living world. Rather than drawing conclusions from a hypothesis and experiment, Goethe suggested that if we just repeatedly and carefully observe nature, insight into natural laws would dawn on us. As farmers and gardeners, this practice of close observation can help us and our crops.

For example, the next time you notice a bug in the garden, don't rush off to read a book by the "experts" to see what it is and how to deal with it. Instead, watch it carefully and see why it's there, what it's doing and eating, what its natural enemies or prey are, what its life cycle is like, and how it relates to the whole environment of your garden. You may be very surprised at what "dawns" on you. Observe and think about what you see, and have confidence in your observations. We're much smarter than the experts would have us believe. We may never know the Latin name for a bug we've observed in this way, but what we learn from this kind of close attention is not as easily forgotten as a paragraph in a book. What we have gained instead of book learning is an internalized knowledge that we can draw on for as long as beans grow in pods.

May 17, 1994

This article was first written as a lecture-meditation given at the Spring 1989 conference of the Tennessee Alternative Growers Association.

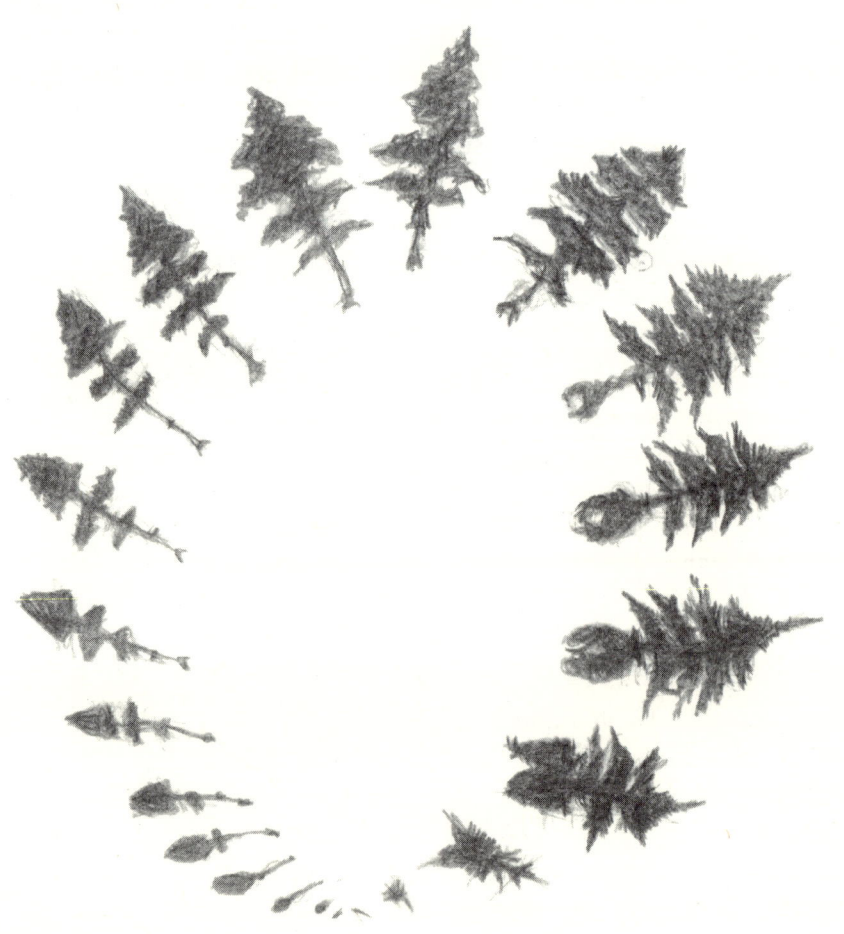

Soil Structure

One of the most frustrating aspects of gardening here in Macon County is the way the soil crusts over after a rain. It packs hard like cement and the little emerging seedlings are obviously having a hard time coming up through it. I am gradually realizing this is the nature of clay soils and a problem of soil structure. If our soils were sandy, we wouldn't have this trouble, but we'd have other ones like low fertility and the soil drying out too fast.

Soil structure is the way that particles of soil hold together. The ideal way is with colloids, which is a term meaning a jelly-like substance; one that is semi-liquid and semi-solid. You can find good soil structure in old fence rows where the land has not been plowed or tramped upon when wet. When you stick a shovel in the ground there and lift it up, the soil looks like chocolate cake or tapioca pudding. It crumbles when you run your hand through it, roots penetrate it and there is life in the soil. It is spongy and has a mat of roots at the surface.

This thatch of roots is the key to understanding soil structure. Roots create soil, not the other way around. It is the constant growing and dying of the grass roots that turns our clay into soil. When the ground is left undisturbed, a slow improvement of the soil structure happens as roots die, decay and form humus. Any kind of tillage destroys soil structure. Once soil structure is mashed, it cannot be made again by us - only roots can do it.

This is hard to believe, because when we work our gardens and farmland, the soil is so much looser afterward. I have taken hard pasture ground, plowed it, and then used a disc to create a fine seed bed. This deceived me into thinking I had improved the ground. After the first rain, when a crust formed, I cursed the clay soil. After years of this, I began to listen to some old-timers who recommended fall plowing with only a light harrowing in spring, rather than creating a fine seed bed in the spring by repeated discing.

My best lessons came from a man who had been raised in Eastern Europe. He talked to me about genuine sustainable agriculture, a way of farming that endured for centuries. It did not involve hauling in pickup loads of manure or bags of fertilizers. First of all, the soil they started with was in good shape. (We will have to do a lot of work just to get to that point.) Secondly, the farm animals were kept off the fields and pastures when it rained. While penned up, their valuable manure was collected. The manure was then mixed with bedding straw and some soil. This mixture was spread on the fields after it had decomposed.

The reason the animals were kept off the wet ground is that they pack it. This was totally unacceptable because the looseness of the soil structure was recognized as being vitally important. They alternated their pasture land with crop land every few years. The mat of roots in the grazed pasture needed to be plowed up. This was done with slow-moving oxen when the soil had just the right moisture content.

The plow had a point on it that would dip into the ground as the ox moved forward. The farmer would lean on the plow handle, the plow would move up and then back down again in a rocking motion. The bottom of the furrow would be anything but an even line. This was all done very slowly, gently turning the sod over, and followed with a light harrowing. Then the seeds were sown. Land treated gently retained its structure and fed people for centuries. I'll never forget the old fellow's advice to plow like you're turning over sleeping babies.

I like to slowly run the rebreaker (also called a chisel plow) in one direction, then wait a week or two and run crossways over the field, making a checkerboard pattern. The delay between working gives the natural processes of decay time to work on the cover crop. If I have to turn a hard fescue sod that the rebreaker won't turn, I use a moldboard plow the first year in the fall when the ground is drier, let the winter frosts work on the rough plowed land and then rebreak it in the spring.

Ideally, you don't want your ground to be pulverized into fine soil too deep, but you want to have larger clumps of soil the deeper you go. This is what is so harmful about rototillers. They make a fine seedbed six or eight inches deep that looks and feels lovely until it rains. Then it packs because the soil structure has been totally pulverized. I've seen small walk-behind tractors with pull-behind implements that are much better for your soil structure than the rotating tines.

The soil is alive, and if we are gentle with it, we can retain soil structure. Then our plants can live on chocolate cake, not cement.

April 5, 1994

Hauling in Manure

Ideas become ideals, but sooner or later they must face the harsh task-maker - reality. The idea is the self-contained farm organism, where everything the farm needs, from feeds to fertilizer, is produced on the farm. The ideal is a rich, black loamy soil growing lush clover and grass pastures that cattle rotate on every few weeks, with the excess cut for winter hay. Fertilizer for the field crops, orchards and gardens comes from their manure. The ideal farm organism would have a balance of animals, meadows and crop land, interspersed with woods and wetlands, and would be able to produce abundantly without external inputs. The produce that leaves the farm is made from carbon, hydrogen, oxygen and nitrogen that the plants have photosynthesized from the sunlight, rain and air which come free to the farm.

The reality is a worn-out, hilly farm with eroded gullies and a hard, acid, clay soil that only wants to grow briars and broom sedge. Although I make many tons of compost during the winter feeding of our cattle, it is just not enough. So I'm admitting an overabundance of idealism and a lack of poop. Last week, James asked me at the feed store if I would clean out a few stalls of his barn that he can't get to with a front-end loader. It's funny how just when you're thinking about something, it turns up.

Cleaning the stalls is a dusty job and the outside tine of the pitchfork keeps bending. But it goes fast, and this manure is so old I just put it on next year's potato field. Normally I compost everything I bring in before I spread it, but this is already very well rotted. On the way to get my fourth load, I run into Terry who asks me if I want to clean his barn. I love coincidences, and it's a sign I need some horse manure. So, while he sharpens my bushhog blades, I load up the pickup with some fine fertilizer.

Another ideal goes out the window, as I spread this, some fairly fresh, onto the field. I don't recommend putting fresh manure on the land for a number of reasons, but here I am doing it. I really want to cover this whole acre, and it's going to take 15 loads, so I'll experiment a little. The trouble is that raw manure releases ammonia nitrate into the soil, causing problems similar to those caused by commercial fertilizers, such as too-quick growth from water-soluble nitrogen. I wouldn't spread fresh manure in the spring, but most of this is somewhat decomposed already and will have all winter to continue rotting.

To hold fast to my ideas of the ideal, self-contained farm organism, I look upon this brought-in manure as a remedy for a sick farm. If the soil was already a fertile humus teeming with life and potential plant growth, it would not need this medication. Our gardens near the house are already in good shape and respond well to a little compost and cover crops. But to expand the farming operation to these worn-out pastures, some imported manure will help speed up the recovery process.

An agriculture that sustains itself must produce its own fertilizer on the farm. Through green manure crops and the proper amount of cattle, fertility can be increased while raising crops. Hauling in feed and fertilizer may work, but we are robbing Peter to pay Paul, and not taking into consideration soil erosion, limited fossil fuels and the environmental consequences of modern farming techniques which have not withstood the test of time.

Holding my ideal in my head, I have something to work toward. Until then, I will help local folks out by cleaning their barns, since no one else wants to do it, and because, as my friend Phil says, "A day hauling manure is a good day."

November 28, 1995

Cover Crops and Crop Rotation

Cover Crops are plants grown specifically for their soil building properties, which is why they are included in our crop rotations. To learn how to best use them, let's look closely at a leaf.

Here in the leaf is where plant growth starts. The first sprouting of a seed is from the energy stored in it, but it is after the first true leaves appear that the plant is really ready to grow. The sun revs up the plant's metabolism as the heart does in our bodies. When the leaf absorbs sunlight, sugars and starches are formed, and when the leaf expands, so do the plant's roots. The roots dig deeper and reach further into the ground, and the plant shoots up, unfolding more leaves. This process continues until the plant flowers.

It is through the earth's canopy of leaves that sun energy is transformed into the raw materials of nature, which we then use and consume. Bare ground is wasteful, which is why Mother Nature loves to send in weeds and why we plant cover crops. Look at a cover crop of rye in late April. Besides what you see above the ground, picture all of those roots underneath the soil surface. Even if you took the above-ground portion off the land, the roots still left are great soil builders. It's double the help when we till in both tops and roots. A live soil will take a few weeks to digest the cover crop once it is turned under. What I worked in three weeks ago is now ready to plant; what I work in today will be ready for a later planting. Here's when the compost, earthworms and soil life really help. By digesting the plant matter, they create new soil quickly.

Rye and wheat are sown in the fall, at about two bushels per acre. These grass-like plants have massive mats of fine roots near the surface and really help to structure the soil. Austrian peas and hairy vetch are nitrogen-producing legumes sown along with the grain at the rate of five to ten pounds per acre. Their deep tap root occupies a different soil layer than the shallow-rooted grasses and helps break up the subsoil. Mixing grains and legumes utilizes their different qualities for soil-building. For a late summer garden, crimson clover is sown the previous fall. It is mown in mid-May when the beautiful red flowers are in bloom. Crimson clover adds nitrogen and leaves the soil loose and in good shape for a June planting of late sweet corn.

When we have a few years to go before we want to crop again, we'll use fescue and clover together. Again, we have the silica-rich grass with its root thatch along with a deep-rooted, calcium-loving legume. I like to inoculate my legume seeds so they'll be sure to have plenty of the bacteria present to form the nitrogen nodules on their roots. White Dutch clover is smaller and used by bees for honey. If you're growing hay, red clover is better because it gets taller. Honeybees don't work red clover, but the blooms are used medicinally. Clover and fescue are sown in the fall and winter months.

Each family of plants performs different functions on our farm, changing the nature of the soil in certain directions. Observing the garden, you'll notice how some crops love to follow others, often ones that use different nutrients and emphasize different parts of the plant. For example, late beans are planted where we grow spring lettuce, and fall kale follows the early beans when they're through in July. By constantly changing crops around, we utilize the individual benefits each family can give to the soil and don't unduly tax our farm's ability to continually produce something. Variety is the spice of life.

In the summer, buckwheat is the star of the cover crops. Its quick growth will smother out weeds and fill in any empty spots in the garden. Buckwheat has the ability to mobilize calcium. When tilled back in, the calcium is more readily available for the next crop. Thomas Jefferson wrote that an acre of buckwheat turned under is worth ten loads of dung. One year, I let a field of buckwheat go to seed and then sprout back up and grow again. Besides helping clear the field of weeds, an amazing thing happened. After frost laid the plants down, I noticed that the soil looked odd. Bending down, I ran it through my fingers. It was earthworm castings; soft, dark and crumbling at the touch. Earthworms had already eaten the first cover crop of buckwheat while the second crop was growing, leaving their rich castings on the soil surface. I learned what a valuable plant buckwheat is.

One time a field of buckwheat rescued a sweet corn patch. It was a dry spring and the seed we had planted in mid-April had not sprouted a bit by mid-May, so I harrowed in some buckwheat for a cover crop because I don't like to leave the land bare. The buckwheat sprouted and grew without any rain at all. About the time it started flowering, still with not a drop of rain, up through the patch came our five rows of sweet corn. The corn seed had not rotted but just sat there in the dry soil. The shallow harrowing didn't disturb it, and when the buckwheat grew it caught enough dew each morning to allow the corn to sprout and grow. The corn was 18 inches tall before I even knew it was there, still in perfect rows, and still without a drop of rain.

Soybean and cowpeas are great legume cover crops, if you can keep deer from eating them. Corn can create a huge mass of organic matter to work back into the ground, and of course, weeds are common cover crops. It is just before the flowering stage that cover crops are best incorporated into the soil. This is when you get the most value for your next crop because the plant hasn't yet put its energy into making seeds.

Traditional agriculture looks at three kinds of crops: soil-building, cultivated and neutral. The soil-builders are grass and clover, the hay and pasture crops. Interestingly enough, they also feed the animals whose manure is invaluable in sustainable agriculture. Cultivated crops deteriorate the land in two ways - through the loss of soil structure by cultivation and the loss of fertility by crop removal. The good things are that they feed us, and by working the ground intensively we get rid of weeds that might invade a long-term pasture. The neutral plants are the grains. Their roots create structure in the soil, but when we harvest the grain we are removing some of the fertility.

Studying the way these groups of plants fed our European ancestors and sustained their soils for centuries sheds light on the importance of crop rotation. After a wheat crop, turnips, cabbage and other late summer crops were sown and kept well cultivated. When they were harvested, the clean field was sown with barley and clover seed. The quick growing barley acted as a nurse crop for the clover, a slow grower. When the barley was harvested for feed, food and beer, the clover took over the field and remained for a couple of years for hay and pasture. Then in the fall the pasture was slowly tilled in and wheat was sown. When it was harvested the following spring, the field was again ready for the cultivation of turnips. In the four-year rotation, soil-builders, cultivated crops and soil structuring grains were all used, following each other and creating a balance. Each farm had four fields, one in turnips to be followed by barley, two in clover to be followed by wheat, and one in wheat to be followed by turnips. The kitchen garden rotated on the clover fields, so potatoes, peas, and carrots were grown in one quarter of the pasture, rotating in such a way that they weren't grown on the same piece of land until 12 years later. Each crop prepares the land for the next one.

On the farms that were leased in England during the 19th Century, the landowners had restrictive clauses in the land leases to protect the soil. For example, it was illegal to grow a grain crop two years in a row on the same field and all land was required to be in at least two years of pasture in the rotation. A most enlightened clause stated that no hay, turnips or straw could be sold from the farm. This meant that the animals fed on these crops could be sold, but not the crops themselves, thus ensuring that fertility would remain on the farm in the form of organic matter, bedding and manures. These leases allowed only the farm's annual excess to be sold and tried to make sure the farm always had land in cover crops and beneficial crop rotations.

April 20, 1999

Forces

I find it interesting to compare the four basic elements with the four kingdoms of nature, the four states of matter, and the four building blocks of life.

Basic Elements	Kingdoms of Nature	States of Matter	Building Blocks of Life
Fire	Human	Warmth	Hydrogen
Air	Animal	Gaseous	Nitrogen
Water	Plant	Liquid	Oxygen
Earth	Mineral	Solid	Carbon

Earth, air, water and fire can be regarded as forces, or energies, that govern nature, matter and life. This ancient way of looking at things can shed light on farm life. The earth element consists of the solid, mineral realm of rocks and other lifeless objects. Carbon is found in everything that once had life, or still does. The water element includes all things that are alive now - the plants and higher kingdoms of nature. All life must have oxygen and water.

The air element encircles our planet above the earth and water. The atmosphere is 80% nitrogen, giving breath and life to the animal kingdom whose sensitivity and mobility differentiate them from rocks and plants. The fire element is epitomized by the sun, which is primarily made up of hydrogen, the lightest atomic element. Humanity's ability for self consciousness, abstract thought and soul work sets them a step above the animal kingdom. (Some human interactions may cause you to doubt this.)

You may notice that each kingdom supplies food for the ones above it and that heat raises each state of matter higher. We eat animals, plants and minerals; the animals eat plants and minerals; and plants live off of the minerals of the earth. From the energy of fire, solid turns to liquid and then to gas. Each kingdom of nature has incorporated the characteristics of the one below. The mineral kingdom is purely physical, but the plant kingdom has life besides. Like plants, animals have both the physical and life bodies, but they also have the ability to feel and sense things. Humans have all of this plus their own personal feeling of selfhood or ego. What does this have to do with farming?

Organic matter is the level of carbon in the garden, and organic gardeners want to keep this level up. Carbon is especially valuable when it also has life, oxygen, with it, because these are all of the living entities in the soil which build humus. The earth and water forces supply the soil with the framework and life our crops depend upon.

Nitrogen is the element that farmers are most concerned about getting on their land for crop production. When we look at nitrogen as the energy of the air, we realize how important the legumes are because they are the plants that breath atmospheric nitrogen into the soil through their symbiotic relationship with certain soil bacteria. Animals, too, give our farms the nitrogen force through their invaluable manure. We can picture nitrogen as being the carrier of what makes animals different from plants, namely desires, instincts and sensations; just as oxygen is the carrier of the life that raises plants above the purely mineral realm.

The sun supplies the warmth that our plants and animals need to grow. When something burns in a fire, only the ashes or earthly carbon compounds remain. The air and water elements have dissipated with the hydrogen energy. Fire sits at the top of the elements just as humans are at the top of the food chain.

Our crops are a combination of carbon, oxygen, nitrogen and hydrogen found as substances in carbohydrates, sugars, starches, fats and protein. These substances are the end product of the processes of the earth, water, air and fire forces. We get these forces in our soils by using cover crops and other plant materials for enriching the earthly carbon with the oxygen or life forces, and with legumes and animal manures for bringing in the air or nitrogen forces. The sun supplies the hydrogen, or fire, energy.

Luckily for us, nature takes good care of these realms. The sun warms up every spring, the rains fall, plants grow out of rocks, worms and insects appear along with other animals to eat the plants and each other, depositing just the right amount of wastes to fertilize more plant growth. The miracles continue season after season, and we get something good to eat with every new day.

July 2, 1996

Lime

Most vegetables and fruits require an adequate amount of lime in the soil to grow well. We limed our fields last week with lime from the mine near Celina rather than from the one near Carthage. To explain why, let's look into the nature of soil pH. The designation "pH," which stands for the "potential of Hydrogen," is the measure of acidity in the soil, with 7 being neutral. A level of 6 is 10 times more acid; a level of 8 is 10 times more alkaline. Most plants like to grow in a soil with pH between 6.2 and 7, so when your soil tests below 6, it is too acid. Since lime is alkaline, you add lime to raise the soil pH. Different limes vary in the amounts of calcium and magnesium they contain and how finely they are ground. It is spread at the rate of one to two tons per acre, every other year or so. Spreading lime affects the balance of cations in the soil, which include several essential nutrients.

Hydrogen is a cation, or positively charged ion. The other cations in the soil are sodium, potassium, magnesium and calcium. These elements create a healthy soil when they are in this particular balance: sodium – less than 1%, potassium – 4-5%, magnesium – 16-18%, calcium – 64-72%. Hydrogen makes up the rest of the percentage, hence the term potential of hydrogen. You'll notice each percentage is four times larger than the one before it, which some nutritionists argue is the most healthy balance of these elements in the human body, as well. My soil tests indicated that we had magnesium levels of 20-30% and calcium levels of only 40-50%. So my magnesium was too high and the calcium too low. I had low pH, so I knew I needed to lime the fields to get rid of broom sedge, get some clover growing, and add essential calcium for the crop land.

Lime is mostly calcium carbonate and magnesium carbonate. Dolomite limestone has a higher magnesium content than regular lime. The lime from Carthage is dolomitic lime and has an analysis that reads "calcium carbonate 48%, magnesium carbonate 32%." This is the lime that had been used on my farm for many years. No wonder I have such a high magnesium level! This lime is 2/5 magnesium. So, I need a lime with a low magnesium level if I want the ratio of calcium to magnesium to get back around four to one.

The lime from Celina has a calcium carbonate level seven times more than its magnesium carbonate level, so I thought it would be better for our soil. Franklin lime from Crab Orchard is an even higher calcium lime, bright white in color, and available in 50 pound bags at some farm supply stores. I wish their mine wasn't so far away, as I've had good results in the garden with it. If your soil test shows a low magnesium level and a high calcium level, I would recommend using the lime from Carthage. Use the best quality lime you can find, but only use dolomite if you are lacking magnesium.

To determine if your garden needs liming, shake a sample of soil in a jar of rainwater and dip a blue litmus paper in it. If it turns pink your soil is acid and you need lime. If a pink litmus strip turns blue, your soil is alkaline.

A heavy clay soil benefits from lime in a number of ways. Toxic aluminum compounds are neutralized, and the texture of the soil is loosened up. Many beneficial soil organisms love lime. But don't add lime directly on manure because it helps the nitrogen fly away as ammonia. On the other hand, rock phosphate spread on manure helps to tie up and save the valuable nitrogen. I don't use quicklime because it robs the soil of water and is harsh on the soil life.

Maintaining a proper pH in the soil is one of the most important tasks facing the farmer. Even when rocks are limestone, the soils are frequently acid. Many of the problems on a farm, from maintaining good stands of clover and hay to crop production and animal health, stem from an imbalance in, or lack of, the major soil cations: calcium, magnesium, potassium and sodium. I am looking forward to seeing the results of using different lime and would love to hear the experiences other farmers are having with lime from Franklin, Celina, Carthage or elsewhere.

October 11, 1994

Subsoiling

The subsoil is the soil that lays underneath the topsoil. On our farm it is usually yellow clay six to twelve inches beneath the surface.

Plant roots love to go deep and many will dive down several feet if they can, but not in compacted soil. Try to picture what's happening underground. Plant roots are growing, looking for water and nutrients. A soil with air spaces makes this much easier. When we plow and cultivate, we bring air into the topsoil. Decaying organic matter, manure and cover crops all help to loosen the topsoil. But the subsoil gets no air. Years of working with the top six to twelve inches have left the subsoil under it compressed into what is called a "hardpan". The hardpan forms right under the plowed land where no tillage happens.

A subsoiler is the farm implement to help remedy this situation. It is a two foot long shank with a two inch wide shoe on the bottom. When the soil is dry, the subsoiler is pulled through the field, digging into the earth beneath the plow layer and into the subsoil, breaking up the hardpan. If the soil is damp, it doesn't do much good, as the moist clay will just squeeze back together. You want the soil to crack and remain open. Actually, some weeds are already doing this. The docks and other indicators of hardpan soils are sending their tap roots down to break up the subsoil. I pull the subsoiler through the field at four foot intervals so the tractor tire doesn't run over the last pass. I like to crisscross the field like a giant tic-tac-toe. My Ford 600 tractor usually can't get the subsoiler in deep enough on the first round, so I'll make another pass and get it in a little deeper. After a few years, the subsoil loosens up and I can get it in two feet deep on the first pass. I constantly have my hand on the lift. When the tires start to slip, I lift it up and when I jerk forward, it goes in deep. I love to crack that subsoil.

Afterwards, we need to get plant roots down in there to keep the soil open. Cover crops and weeds send their roots into the cracks and when they die and rot, they leave organic matter and airspace in those lower soil layers. Topsoil falls into the cracks and helps keep it open. Sometimes I put lime over the opening and then run the subsoiler over it to work it down in. Plant roots don't like the acid subsoil, but if we can sweeten it and open it up, the roots can get in there and have some fun.

Just think of all the plant nutrients and soil moisture under the topsoil that are unavailable to plants. When we start working with our subsoil, we can double the amount of land we are using right there on the same spot. It is a slow process. Our five-inch topsoil layer may get to be six inches in a few years, with the cracks going down 12 or 15 inches. But in another few years, we can have 24 inches of soil moisture and nutrients available for our plants and get our topsoil to really interact and breathe with the subsoil.

In the kitchen garden, we aerate the subsoil by double-digging the beds. I remove a few shovelfuls of top soil and thrust the digging fork into the subsoil to wiggle around and loosen it up. Once the plant roots get in deep, they will keep the soil open, as long as we don't create hardpan again with poor plowing practices. It's a natural process of the soil, getting better and better as plant roots die and turn into soil at ever-deeper levels. We just need to help them crack that subsoil so they can get started.

September 12, 1995

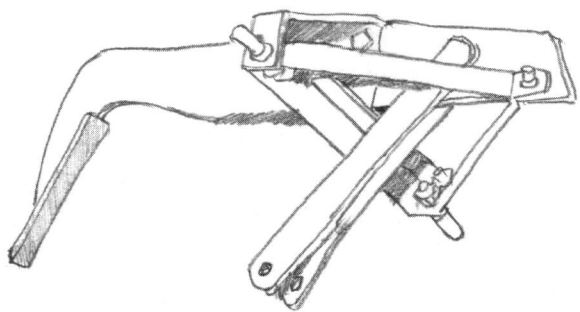

Manure Spreader

The manure spreader is the implement of choice for getting compost from the piles to the fields. When I moved up to it from the pitchfork, the farm took a quantum leap forward. The last few springs have been so wet that the window of opportunity for getting the ground composted, tilled and planted was smaller than the jobs at hand. Consequently, I planted some of the early crops too late. So this fall finds me hooking the spreader to the tractor and off to get the future pea, onion and potato beds composted. After four successful loads, the lever for the spinner sticks. Looks like it's back to the pitchfork.

I pull the manure spreader into the orchard and bless the lovely pears and a few apple trees with a ring of biodynamic compost. They thank me just by looking better with the black-gold underneath their bare branches. Back at the barn, I take the wheel and gear off and formulate this golden rule: "When the zerk won't take grease, you will have problems." A zerk is an alemite, or grease fitting, and the one in question is not allowing grease to reach an important bearing, which, in turn, was not allowing the lever to move freely. Ignoring this got me here today. Actually, the zerk turns out to be fine after I poke the dried grease out from behind it. Charles came by and we found a few more potential problems. I temporarily rob some zerks off my old tractor, and it sure feels good to get grease into some very greaseless places.

This manure spreader changed my life. Ten years ago, I saw it for sale for $250. I'd always been shy of overly mechanical things, and this was that. Gears and chains and sprockets adorned it. But until now it had never given me a lick of trouble and has helped turn our organic garden into an organic farm. I've gradually become more mechanized ever since.

One lever engages a chain which pulls the compost to the back of the machine. It has five different settings for five different application rates. I use the low one for pastures and the upper settings for the heavier feeding crops. Ours is a wheel-driven model. Some manure spreaders are driven from the PTO (power take off), which is handy for making compost. You just fill it up with the raw materials, and it mixes everything and leaves it in a nice neat windrow.

The other lever (the one that got stuck) gets the spinners whizzing. They pick up the compost, chop it up, and fling it as you drive over the field. The faster you go, the farther it flings. To make a bed, I drive slowly so that all the compost lands right behind the spreader in a neat four foot-wide row. I like to work the compost into the soil soon after it is spread so it doesn't dry out. I roll faster over the rye and Austrian pea cover crop, flinging compost far and wide. There's not much I'd rather do than spread compost on the garden. (As I was scraping the last little bit of it out of Charles' front end loader, he had to agree, it'd be hard to find someone who likes manure as much as I do.)

Compost enlivens the soil in many ways. Besides the N-P-K, it also supplies the ground with trace elements and minerals. But best of all, it's teeming with the invisible benefactors such as bacteria, enzymes and the other microorganisms that play such an important role underground. It acts as a catalyst to bring about beneficial activity, most notably the formation of stable humus. A rich humus soil will withstand adverse weather conditions much better than a non-humus soil. The food tastes better, too, as any cow will tell you. Watch where they first graze on a new pasture, and you'll find your best soil there.

The manure spreader is a valuable part of the farm. I was glad to finally give mine a little more attention. Luckily the job was forced on me now and not during a mad rush in spring. I did pull out an oak branch while forking compost on those pear trees, which could have damaged the spreader if chance hadn't stuck the lever and found me pitch-forking. It's great how things are always working out for the best, even when it seems they are not. Is chance an angel?

December 1, 1998

Marketing

Marketing is a key to any successful business venture, and truck farming is no exception. We've been fortunate that the demand for organic produce has grown as our farm production has increased. We started trading extra garden vegetables in the late 70's to our friends and neighbors. We were organic, but I can't recall anyone caring much about that. They just wanted homegrown produce.

In the early 80's, we tried a tomato crop and, living in a rural community, couldn't give tomatoes away. When we had vegetables, everyone had them. So we took some to a small health food store, Sunshine Grocery in Nashville, and met their produce manager, Tom. He was pleased to learn that there was an organic farm in Tennessee and bought all we brought him most of the time. His major complaint was lack of consistency. He wanted all the heads of lettuce to weigh the same, the potatoes to be the same size and none of those odd-shaped squash. Vegetable sorting became a new farm chore. By the end of the 80's, we were sorting five tons of potatoes into three different grades - culls, small and large.

The Corner Market in West Nashville had just opened, and we started moving produce there. Our friend Rory, who ran the club where our rock'n'roll band played, started working at The Corner Market as the produce manager just as the demand for organic vegetables skyrocketed. Meanwhile, Sunshine Grocery opened a supermarket on Belmont Avenue, full of natural products and boasting a huge produce section. Tom was shipping in organic produce by the truckload from California, and paying high prices. "I'll give you the same price if you give me the same quality," he told me, so quality control had to gear up on the farm. Luckily, at the same time, we were gathering a group of loyal, local friends and customers who wanted to support our organic farm.

More and more folks were not happy with modern agriculture's dependence on artificial fertilizers, pesticides and herbicides. Slowly but surely, people were realizing these things were not healthy for them or the soil. As we stepped up the quality of what we shipped out, we had a surplus of "seconds". These we offered to our friends at a much cheaper price or for free if they wanted to pitch in a day or two each year at planting or harvest time. So when an acre of potatoes needs to be planted or dug, I call around and get a few hands to make the job easier and more fun. In exchange, several families get free vegetables, which may be "seconds" to the stores, but are perfectly good to eat.

There are many people who are sensitive to chemicals used on their food. They need the assurance that our produce has not been sprayed, so we have a national organic certification agency check our farm out every year. In 1997, we obtained a restraining order from the courts to halt the aerial spraying of herbicides along transmission lines throughout the county. Although we backed down when the utility company threatened to countersue, they've never sprayed near our farm and have promised not to. We received enormous emotional support from a wide variety of folks, because most people just don't like the idea of spraying poisons.

Knoxville Food Co-op is a membership-owned grocery store that always takes a few truckloads of our vegetables each year. I try to combine a trip over there with visiting my family in the Smoky Mountains. Our prices to the health food stores have remained about the same for 10 years. We set them at a level where we will want to grow the crop again, or often just let Tom and Rory set the price at what they'd have to give to get the same quality elsewhere.

Our produce is also available by mail order. We pack boxes of sweet potatoes, garlic, butternuts and Irish potatoes and send them all over the country. A group, Spiritual Food for the New Millennium, operating out of Maryland, organizes this, and the produce can be ordered through them. In the nursery business I sent fruit trees using UPS, so I'm used to the mail order business, but it's a far cry from selling locally. Still, I appreciate folks wanting to support biodynamic farms in this way.

Another important market for us several years ago was a Community Supported Agriculture (CSA) venture near Chattanooga. Alex had organic gardens full of lettuce, beans, tomatoes and other vegetables that he supplied to 30 families who, in turn, covered the annual budget he submitted to them each spring. In other words, they all bought a share of the garden before it was even planted. Along with his own produce, he offered them shares of potatoes, butternuts and sweet potatoes from us since his garden wasn't big enough for these crops.

We now have our own CSA with 32 members. Driver Dan shows up every Monday at noon and backs up to our cave, where we have baskets and boxes filled with the freshly-harvested produce. He carries the food to Nashville where Gabrielle and another member or two divide the bulk produce into individual boxes. She takes care of all the customers, phone calls and payment collection. We charge our CSA members $100 per month or $25 per week, and members are free to drop out at any time, though few do. The response has been highly favorable.

The main criteria for joining is "to eat like I eat". The first few shipments in May were peas, lettuce and onions. Soon, we were sending garlic, summer squash, beets, carrots, green beans, dill, parsley and other spring and summer vegetables and herbs. Later in the year, the members received tomatoes, potatoes, melons and sweet corn. In the fall, leeks, peppers, sweet potatoes, butternuts and leafy vegetables, including an assortment of oriental greens, collards, kale, daikons and turnips filled the boxes. Our members canned tomatoes and beans, froze sweet corn, and made pesto from the excess sweet basil. There was an abundance of food in the garden, and it was so nice for me to not have to worry about what to do with it. We just cleaned out the garden every Monday morning and sent it off. In our last few shipments in December we were running low on veggies, so we included freshly-ground corn meal, homemade Christmas wreaths and bottles of homemade wine.

Our members get something else besides the produce. They have a chance to care for a piece of land. We have always encouraged folks to come out for a family picnic, a hike through the forest, or a camp-out. The kids can watch baby calves play, swim in the creek, and see the gardens growing the food they'll soon be eating.

Community Supported Agriculture (I love the sound of that name) seems like a solution to many of the world's problems by reinvigorating rural areas with thriving gardens and getting fresh food directly to consumers. CSA's could interrelate so families could get dairy, meat, breads, fruits and vegetables all straight from the farms. People living within the rhythms of the seasons would feel more connected to the earth and nature and have a sense of satisfaction in supporting healthful farms.

In Tennessee and Kentucky the tobacco allotment program, which is now being dismantled, has saved many small farms and rural communities by insuring a market for a labor-intensive crop. CSAs now offer another way to save small family farms, this time by a group of families meeting the farm's financial needs in exchange for the farm's produce. Instead of grossing $15,000 from a few acres of tobacco, a farmer planting vegetables can gross the same amount having 30 families give $25 a week for 20 weeks. By extending the season or feeding more families, or both, the income could be greatly increased. Farmers don't need subsidies, just fair prices.

The modern trend of semi-trucking food across the country, fast food, junk food and poor health from poor eating could be replaced by local gardens and farms producing abundant quality food. Farmers would make their decisions based on their spiritual insight and intuition of what's best for their land, improving the natural environment without having to fret about money. In time, more young people would be attracted to farming as viable life work. With each farmer feeding 30 to 40 people or families, those not farming would still do their other jobs yet develop a closeness to the earth, helping their decision-making in various realms to be more earth-friendly.

September 9, 1997

Chamomile

Asteraceae   Matricaria chamomilla

CHAPTER II

Spring into Action

Seeds	37
Companion Planting	39
Peas	41
Onions	44
Carrots	46
Parsley	48
Potatoes	50
Harrowing	53
Asparagus and Rhubarb	55
Wildflower Hike	57
Hoeing	59

"Let us cultivate our gardens."

Voltaire

Seeds

The seed is an article of faith. As gardeners, we put our trust in the seeds we plant, knowing that from such small beginnings come all the wealth of our crops. Most seeds are planted directly outdoors, but sometimes we can treat them for quicker germination. Other seeds are sown in flats to raise plants to set out in the garden later.

Pea, beet, and other early crop seeds can be soaked in lukewarm water overnight before planting, to ensure better sprouting once they are in the cool spring ground. Aged compost can be added to the water to make a fertilizing tea. As the seed swells, it soaks up the tea and gets off to a healthy start. Hard seeds, such as okra and some of the flower seeds (moonflower vine, for example), are best soaked before sowing. Many tree seeds even need to be nicked, that is, filed through the hard shell so the kernel can get moisture to sprout. I think many seeds need to be frozen and thawed for best germination. One year I saved my best soybeans in a jar inside the house, and they didn't sprout well when I planted them. It was such a thin stand I hoed it up and replanted with some soybeans that had been sitting in a bushel basket outside all winter, and they all came up.

We are trying something new with our potato seed this year, an old English custom called "chitting." We placed the potatoes stem end down and seed end up in shallow trays (cardboard boxes cut off at two inches tall) upstairs in our house. The warm temperature will get the potatoes sprouting, but the indirect light will keep the sprouts green and stubby. Besides getting an early crop, this method is supposed to increase yields. As it has been too wet to work in the fields, chitting the potatoes has relieved my anxiety about not having them planted yet.

To start tomatoes, peppers, cabbages, onions and flowers, we mix up our own potting soil. We stir about 1/3 sand, 1/3 compost, and 1/3 soil in a wheelbarrow with some lime and rock phosphate. We put this mixture into shallow plastic trays with holes in the bottom, and sow the seeds in rows two inches apart. Transplanting happens after the plants have gotten their first true leaves. The cabbage plants and slender onion slips are set out directly in the garden.

The tomatoes and peppers will get transplanted into soil blocks. We used to transplant them into little paper or plastic cups, and then found an easier way using a tool called a "soil blocker." It makes little two-inch square blocks with a hole in the top for the plant to go in. Take some of the potting soil, dampen it, then press out the blocks, and, amazingly, they stick together. Then the blocks are put in a cold frame until all danger of frost is past and the seedlings are big enough to set out in the garden. It also works well to simply plant seeds directly into the cold frame soil, about two or three inches apart, where they grow until it's warm enough for them to be safely planted outside. Excess watering causes damping off problems, so let the roots run deep and water thoroughly but infrequently.

Seeds are truly a wonder. It's awesome to look at such a little thing and think of all the possibilities. First, the root shoots down, and the sprout breaks the ground. Then leaf after leaf unfolds, and the plant grows up towards the sun. With the interaction of soil life and minerals underground and the insect world in the air, the plant will flower and bear a crop of seeds many times more than what was started with.

I'm reading Henry David Thoreau's newly published manuscript, "The Dispersion of Seeds", a scientific work included in the book, <u>Faith in a Seed</u>. I love to see science and art bridged together in such a spiritual way. Thoreau quotes an experiment by Darwin in which he took three tablespoons of pond mud and kept it in his study for six months, pulling up and counting each plant as it grew. Many different kinds of plants sprouted up. Altogether, there were 537 of them. Another note Thoreau made was that if a single thistle seed sprouted and bore a crop, and each seed did the same, after just five generations there would be more than a sufficient number of plants to stock not only the surface of the earth, but also all of the planets in the solar system. There would be no room for anything else, allowing one square foot for each plant.

Seeds are everywhere and productive beyond belief. I can look at all of humanity's inventions and still find more miracles and power hidden in a single seed.

April 9, 1996

Companion Planting

Companion planting is the practice of growing different plants next to each other because observation has shown they grow better together. Just as people have mutual attractions, so does the plant world. The best known combination is beans, corn and pumpkins, the three sisters that the Native Americans were growing together when European settlers arrived. We put pumpkins in our corn patch every year, but on the earlier patches I wait to plant the pumpkins until after the corn is up so they don't smother the small corn plants. The pumpkin leaves shade the ground and conserve moisture for the corn, and the corn doesn't slow down the pumpkins. Cornfield beans, or any other climbing bean, can be sown in the corn rows to climb up the stalks; as legumes, they add nitrogen to the soil that the corn needs. The fibrous shallow corn roots occupy a different soil layer than the deeper taproots of the bean or pumpkin plants.

Beans like to grow around carrots, beets and cabbages also, but do not like onions and garlic. We have garlic sprouting up wherever there was an old garlic crop. Its strong odor is bound to be helpful around fruit trees and roses to deter pests. Potatoes and beans can be sown in alternate rows. The beans repel the Colorado potato beetle, and the potatoes repel the Mexican bean beetle.

Cucumbers, potatoes and cabbage appreciate a little shade from nearby corn or trellised peas and beans. We sprinkled radish seeds in squash rows to repel the cucumber beetle this year. Lettuce and carrots grow well together and combine well in the salad bowl, too. Both like radishes, and all are planted about the same time in the early spring. The cabbage family likes beets and potatoes, and especially aromatic herbs and flowers. Peppers don't like tomatoes and zucchini doesn't either.

Most herbs are beneficial in the garden. Dill, chamomile, basil, sage, chives, rosemary, thyme and parsley all have a good effect on neighboring plants. Their aromas and flowers add another dimension to the garden, drawing in helpful insects and bees. Lemon balm, peppermint, yarrow, hyssop, marjoram, lavender and many others all have special properties that would be worth exploring. Exactly why some plants like each other is not fully understood. It could be the aromas or root secretions, or maybe the insects they attract or repel. Fennel and wormwood are the exception here. Most plants do not like to grow near them.

Flowers also have a place in the garden. Marigolds excrete something from their roots that repels nematodes, so they get a place in our rose garden. We also plant marigolds with muskmelons, and tomatoes are said to bear better fruit with marigolds in the rows. Nasturtiums repel the squash bug and aphids. Tansy or pennyroyal planted around the doorsteps will keep ants out of the house.

Besides general likes and dislikes that plants have, experience has shown other handy combinations. A watermelon patch has a lot of empty space in it for the first couple of months and can grow quick crops like bush beans and lettuce, which will be gone by the time the vines get going. Summer lettuce grows well where the beech tree gives afternoon shade. Just as we work and feel best around our friends, plants will grow better in their preferred company. As we are the seed-sowers, it is up to us to carefully observe how our plants are doing and to learn all we can about them.

June 6, 1995

Peas

Peas are the first seeds to get planted in our garden every spring. There is nothing much sweeter than fresh garden peas, and they are easy to grow. It's best to have your pea patch prepared in the previous fall. Peas don't like to grow where they were grown the year before. Like other members of the legume family, peas appreciate lime worked into the soil a few months before they are planted. I did get some lime out last fall, but the spot for the peas was still in sod when I ran the chisel plow through it in February. Another pass in early March loosened up the clumps of grass enough so that I could get in with a garden fork and remove them.

My garden fork is one of my favorite tools. The heavy-duty tines are so big they never bend, and the four of them will take care of anything that needs digging. I tossed the grass clumps to the side. They'll either rot there or make it to a compost pile. Old timers used to pile grass clumps this time of year, layered with manure, to make potting soil for next spring. I spread several bushels of compost on about 200 feet of pea rows and then worked it in. A hoe made an inch and a half deep furrow, and we were about ready to plant.

First, we sprinkled a legume inoculant on the slightly moistened pea seeds. This is a black powder with the bacteria in it that grows on the pea roots and fixes nitrogen from the air. You can pull up a pea plant later in the year and see little white balls on the roots. Although peas take other nutrients to grow, they leave behind these beads of nitrogen for the next crop. Soil from an old pea patch will have the bacteria in it, too. We find it easier to use the inoculant though, so we don't have to move old soil around.

We have in the past placed pea seed the recommended two inches apart, and when they came up they made a very pretty row of plants. But now I just sprinkle the seed in the row and let them grow up as they will. Peas don't need thinning and seem to like to grow thickly. Peas are also forgiving about rough soil. If it's too wet at planting time to really pulverize the soil, they just get planted into a lightly prepared row. I spread a pickup load of compost over the bed after we have covered the rows. This will help keep the soil from crusting over the top, and the peas will love it later on as the earthworms work it into the ground for us. Mid-March is almost too late for pea planting, but I have lost February sowings to cold snaps. Peas are a cool weather crop that can withstand frosts but not a prolonged 20 degree spell. They need to be in early because they peter out when hot weather arrives.

I rake over the pea row before the seedlings emerge to kill germinating weed seeds. After a few cultivations they are ready to be staked. Any old woven wire fence works well, with tobacco sticks hammered in the ground every ten feet for support. Cattle panels are also excellent for this use. These 16' long, four foot tall welded steel panels are available at farm supply stores. But even branches will give enough for the peas to climb on. One hand-hoeing at this point will suffice. Because the peas grow so fast, they'll shade out the weeds. After harvest the pea vines can be removed, and a row of late climbing plants, like luffa sponges or pole beans, can go in the same spot.

Sugar snaps, a snow pea with plump peas inside, are our favorite snack in June. Crisp, juicy and sweet, they are also prolific and much taller than English peas. The five or six foot tall vines are good at climbing but tend to fall over in the wind and rain. The last few years I've dealt with this problem by putting the pea fence to one side of the row and slightly leaning it. When the peas climb it and start flowering, I weave bamboo cane poles in at about three feet above the ground to keep the vines from falling over when they get full of peas.

English peas, on the other hand, hold to the trellis better and only get about three feet tall. Green Arrow is the pea we grow for shelled peas. The abundant 5 inch long pods are well-filled and delicious. Peas make a beautiful plant that has been grown for centuries in European gardens. Sweet peas are grown just for their pretty flowers and the flat-podded snow peas are a Chinese delicacy.

The leaves of peas are edible, too, and add a great flavor to early spring salads. Raw peas are so good it's a wonder we ever cook them at all. But slightly steamed up with some new potatoes and baby carrots, they will put you in a late spring heaven. We can the mature peas in pint jars to stock up in the cellar. One or two mid-June days will find a pea-shelling party on our front porch. Next year I'll try and get my pea ground prepared in the fall. They need an early start, as the hot weather wipes them out. The spring garden starts with peas, and it's a sweet beginning.

March 25, 1997

Onions

Onions are early and easy. Fresh green ones are ready a few weeks after planting sets, and a good bulb will store all winter. As soon as you can work the ground in the spring it is time to plant onion sets. These are small onions grown from seed last year, but grown in poor soil so they'll stay small. The onion is a biennial plant, which means it flowers and bears seed in its second year. So a small onion set will grow fast in the spring, but it may send up a flower stalk. This is a hard stalk in your onion, lessening its appeal and storage life. The onions that don't send up flower stalks will keep longer.

I've grown onions many different ways. Our main problems are that they don't shade out the weeds so they require a lot of hoeing, and many of them rot. I had a small success one year planting the sets and immediately mulching with hay, but that was a dry spring. The next spring was a wet one, and the mulched onions all rotted. They seem to like dryness to a certain degree. Although they need the spring rains to grow, dry weather later on helps keep them from rotting in the field. This week I manured and chisel plowed last fall's turnip patch and made four 200 foot rows with a wide hoe. Yellow Ebenezer onion sets were planted every three or four inches in the row and then covered about one inch deep. I usually plant 30 pounds of yellow onion sets, but this time I set out some white onion sets and put out only 15 pounds of yellows.

I'll rake over the rows a week after planting and keep the rows weeded. When the tops start dying back in late June or early July, we'll pull them and let them dry in the field for a few days before gently laying them up in the hay loft. I think rough handling makes for bruises that reduce their keeping quality. After they are thoroughly dry, we tie them in bunches and hang them up in the loft. When it starts freezing hard in November, we hang them in the chicken coop, where the heat from the hens is just enough to keep the coop from freezing near the insulated ceiling. We still lose onions to rot along the way, so the last few years we've been trying to grow them from seed. We grew some beautiful red ones called Torpedo that were oblong and delicious, but they did not keep well.

When you look for onion seed, the package will say either "long day onions" or "short day onions". This refers to the days' length in summer when the onions are maturing. As summer days are longer in the North, Northern gardeners grow long day onions, while Southern folks need short day onions. The Parks seed catalog offers four short day Southern onion varieties, and, of course, we have to try them all; Yellow Granex, Red Granex, Sweet Georgia Brown and Tropea Tonda Red. We're also trying Texas Grano, but many have already died from damping off, so we're not too impressed.

Seeds are sown in flats filled with sand, compost and soil. They are slow to grow and are so wimpy it's hard to believe they'll ever do anything. We'll transplant them out in a garden bed in April and dutifully hoe them, pulling the soil away from the larger plants later in the year so half of the bulb is above ground level. Onions from seed do not send up flower stalks the first year. Hence, they make better bulbs for storing, as the plant will want to be alive to send up a flower stalk the following year. We've noticed the onions with the smaller necks store the best.

My grandma used to stomp on the onions in the field, claiming this made for bigger bulbs. My father, on the other hand, never did appreciate having all his onions tromped.

Nest onions are an interesting plant. They form little sets off to the side that can be planted as onion sets in the spring and make green onions, too. The walking onion, which reaches a height of three feet, makes bulblets on its flower stalk that fall over and sprout, thus "walking" about three feet per year. We've grown King Richard leeks by planting the slips four inches deep, then hilling them up during cultivation to make long, sweet white leeks. These delicious milder onions are a prime ingredient in potato and leek soup and are fine additions to salads, too.

I've dug a trench, filled it with onions that obviously weren't going to store in the fall, and had early green onions the next spring. Onions are edible all year from the bulb on up, and they sure make a mess of 'taters or beans a little livelier.

April 1, 1997

Carrots

What's up, Doc? Carrots are up and in, and there is nothing much better for a crunchy snack which is so nutritious and takes up so little space. My first gardening experiences with carrots were dismal failures, producing only short, stubby, bland roots. Then I learned the carrot secret: sand. Just as leaf and fruit crops have an affinity for calcium, that most soft and soluble element, the root crops like to grow around hard and insoluble silica. Although silica is not water-soluble, all plants need it, especially the root crops.

Silica makes up almost one-half of the earth's crust, mostly in the form of common sand. Silica crystals are used in radio receivers and silicon chips store information in computers. The clear crystals of sand are somehow very important for plant growth. The silica in a fruit or root's skin helps it to store better. On the other hand, a lack of silica will make food spoil more quickly. In African villages, traditionally-raised wheat straw is used as a thatch for roofs. These roofs lasted twenty years or more because of their high silica content. Modern farming techniques have given higher yields, but the thatch from artificially fertilized wheat straw will last only three to five years. When analyzed, this straw shows a high potassium content, but low silica. The plants were taking in the water-soluble potassium fertilizer and not absorbing silica from the soil, and the final product rotted faster.

Back to the carrot bed. I took a couple of ten foot sassafras 1x8's and nailed them to a couple of five foot 1x8's to make a rectangle. I did this again and set the second frame on top of the first one, creating a 16 inch deep box that measures ten feet by five feet. About half of this was filled with sand from near the creek, and the other half was filled with good garden soil and compost. It was all mixed together with some rock phosphate and sown with Bolero and Touchan carrots in February, making five rows about ten inches apart. These two varieties seem fairly resistant to alternaria blight, which can turn carrot tops black. I also like the Danvers and the Nantes type carrots.

On some of our better garden soil, I just poured a few buckets of sand and that's where we're getting carrots now. These were sown in March, and I'll plant a fall carrot bed in late July. Carrots are slow growers at first, and the sand really makes pulling weeds easier. Old farming books say the best thing to add to clay soils is sand, just as in sandy soils they recommend adding clay. It is the mixture of large, hard sand particles and small, soft clay particles that make loam, the ideal soil. Bugs don't bother carrots at all, although every now and then a beautiful green and yellow caterpillar has to be taken somewhere else to eat and turn into a black swallowtail butterfly.

We thin carrots to an inch or two apart in their row, and keep them weeded. In salads, soups and casseroles, carrots add a lovely bright color and delicious flavor. Homegrown carrots are very sweet and are rich in vitamin A. The wild carrot is common on our farm, blooming in June with its white, Queen Anne's lace flower. Cut them down if you want to save your own carrot seed; otherwise, leave them, because beneficial insects love them.

Over the years, I've come to love the sandy spots in the garden where I've grown carrots. Unlike sawdust and other organic mulches that we use to loosen our heavy clay soils, sand doesn't decay and is a permanent addition. Beets, parsnips and other garden roots appreciate growing in an old carrot bed. Carrots are easy to grow once you've learned their sandy secret, and as you crunch on a bright orange root waving its lacy green leaves around, you may indeed feel a little like Bugs Bunny.

June 27, 1995

Parsley

Parsley is one of those plants that's easy to take for granted. I eat it almost every day and hardly ever give it a second thought. With the Red Boiling Springs Folk Medicine Festival this weekend, I wanted to write about an herb. But the more I think about parsley, the fuzzier the distinction between an herb and a vegetable becomes. The word "herb" implies medicinal properties as well as a flavoring, but all vegetables raised organically have great flavor and are good for you. We chop up a handful of parsley in our daily salad. More than just a seasoning, it is famous for its high vitamin content and fresh flavor. Food is our medicine, and medicine is our food.

Parsley seed is slow to germinate. We used to start it in flats indoors with the other herbs and set the plants out a foot apart in the herb bed. But for the last few years I've been direct-sowing it into the garden in rows eighteen inches apart in early spring. Three weeks later, slender leaves sprout and soon the characteristic foliage appears, allowing me to tell the parsley from the weeds. We don't even thin it anymore, just let it grow up thickly in the row. It fills up the space, and all summer long we have a healthy parsley patch for soups and salads. I cut it with a sharp knife about three inches above the crown and it quickly grows right back up. It sells for about $8.00 a pound, or 60¢ a bunch.

Like all leaf crops, parsley loves a rich soil and plenty of compost. It grows when it rains and tolerates the dry weather better than other crops, probably because of its deep tap root. The feathery, finely serrated leaves speak of the light forces at work and a strong silica presence, which accounts for parsley's nutritious qualities. I added sand to the parsley bed this year, and it's as good a patch as I've ever grown. Italian Giant is the biggest variety we grow, with a flat leaf and longer stem. Dwarf Curly and Green River seem identical to me. They are the curly-leafed parsleys that commonly garnish your dinner at a restaurant. I can't taste the difference in any of the varieties, but we like the texture of the curly better.

In the fall, we carefully dig up a few plants and transplant them into the greenhouse bed. They wilt back some, but soon regain their hold on the earth and grow great all winter long. With the low winter light, they make more stems and fewer leaves, but they still supply us with fresh parsley until next spring's crop is ready to nibble on. Parsley is a biennial; it lives for two years, making seeds the second year. I let some stay in the garden over the winter a few years ago, and when it sent up its seed stalk I collected the seeds. I planted them too late this year, just in time for a spring drought. Nothing came up, so I'll have to try that again sometime. Parsley seed is not very viable, meaning it doesn't store well. It is an Old World crop, grown in Europe for many centuries. It is a staple in their diets there, and they have recipes that call for parsley root. It is a relative of celery, which, when you think about it, looks like an expanded parsley plant. The same family of plants, *Umbelliferae*, includes carrots, fennel, dill and yarrow. They are all aromatic with finely laced leaves and deep roots.

We harvest parsley and hang it upside down in the attic to dry for parsley flakes. This year, we put some in the solar oven that we use for drying vegetables, and in a few hours it was dry enough to store, retaining its vibrant, bright green color. The curly leaf parsley is a beautiful plant and makes a lovely border around the herb bed or vegetable garden. So whether you use it as a seasoning, medicine, vegetable, garnish, or just as a pretty plant to look at, parsley has a place in the garden.

July 23, 1996

Potatoes

When we first started gardening here, we didn't raise potatoes because they were so cheap at the store. Of course, when we did grow a few rows, we were overwhelmed by how much better tasting they were, so the next year we decided to plant 50 pounds. At the time, in the mid-seventies, I was getting Organic Gardening magazine, and they had an article on mulching with leaves. Great idea, I thought. I worked up some ground, laid off the rows with our mare Nellie, planted the potatoes, and covered them with a good thick layer of leaves. Well, like so many of my good ideas, this one wasn't so good. The leaves rotted and packed, and the potatoes couldn't grow very well. When we dug them we barely got our 50 pounds back. I should have chopped the leaves up first.

So the next year I let my neighbor Wayne teach me how to grow spuds the Macon County way, and we've had good crops ever since. After a heavy composting, rows are made with a hoe or plow, two to three inches deep. Spuds smaller than the size of a hen's egg are left whole, others are cut once or twice to about that size, always leaving a couple of eyes in each piece. Then they are dropped a foot apart and covered up. Potatoes resprout if they get frosted so can be sown in mid-March to take advantage of the cooler weather that they like.

Raking over the rows before they come up, which takes three weeks or so, gets rid of the young weeds, and hilling them as they grow is beneficial. Walking down the row knocking potato beetles into a bucket is a summer chore that ends at the pond, to feed the fish and cool off. We wait a few weeks after the plants die before we dig them, so the skins will cure and they'll store better.

I haven't given up potato experimenting, though. I got to wondering about varieties, so I planted a patch with 18 different kinds of potatoes one year: yellow ones, blue ones, Burbanks, Russets - potato varieties from Maine to Peru. Lo and behold, the ones that did the best, by far, were Kennebec and Red Pontiac from the Red Boiling Springs feed store.

Potatoes can be planted on rich soil and then covered with a mulch. One year we mulched 1/4 acre of potatoes with hay and 1/4 acre with wheat straw, and the difference was clear. The potatoes under hay did exceptionally well, but the plants with the straw were quite yellow and weak. Straw usually has no weed seeds and is a good soil builder, but robs more nitrogen from the soil than hay does because it has a higher carbon to nitrogen ratio. It stole from our potato patch.

In last year's experiments, I learned some important lessons about soil structure. I had long thought of the soil as alive, as I quickly plowed, disced, and otherwise pulverized it into shape for planting, but I hadn't really been treating it as though it was alive. The first rain would turn my fine soil into cement and form a crust over the surface.

But two falls ago, I plowed v-e-r-y s-l-o-w-l-y. It took all afternoon to plow two acres, going as slowly as I could, and only four to five inches deep. In the spring, I ran the rebreaker with a harrow crossways across the field, again very slowly, and then waited a week or so before rebreaking it in the direction I had plowed in the fall. The land was anything but ready to plant, still rough and full of sod, but I planted an acre of potatoes anyway. Three weeks later, I had a beautiful lawn and no potatoes. But, amazingly, the ground was still soft. The potatoes eventually came up, and I cultivated them, again very slowly, and the grass between the rows was taken care of as the tines of the cultivator broke up the clods. After every rain, all my other fields packed hard as usual, but this potato field always stayed nice and soft. For the first time, I hadn't ruined the soil structure.

My yields were less than the year before, which had been a great potato year in a field that was much more fertile than this one. But I was happy with the results, because when the potato beetles came they didn't do nearly the damage they usually do. Something about the soil structure must have made the plants less susceptible to the beetles. All that careful, slow cultivation had paid off in the pest area. I followed the potatoes with buckwheat, planted in July, a beautiful cover crop I highly recommend. Then I inter-sowed rye and vetch for a winter cover crop, still retaining the soil structure. Unfortunately, the electric fence didn't keep my cattle out. The rye and vetch looked good and green from their side of the fence, and they got in and tromped it. Pasturing the cows near this field was another one of those not-so-good ideas, I guess. Although cattle are necessary for sustainable agriculture, a whole herd of them on your garden is not a pretty sight. The ground recovered well, but I've lost my trust in pasturing cows near a garden.

March 22, 1994

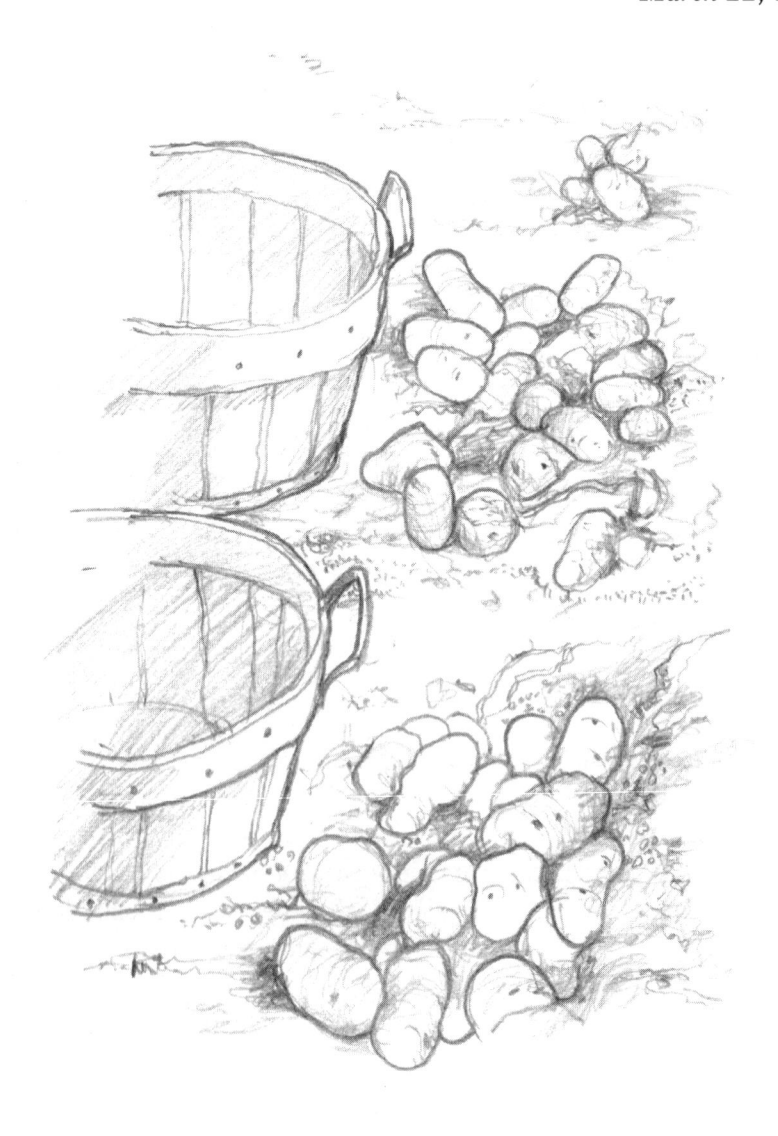

Harrowing

I've had a harrowing experience this week. I have three different types of harrows: a disc harrow, a spike-tooth harrow and a spring-tooth harrow, but I only used the latter two this week. In farming, the old saying is really true - you need the right tool for the job. The disc is a great tool for working in corn stalks and other vegetable matter in late summer, but I have really damaged soil structure by using it on freshly plowed ground in the spring.

Where I grew up, in Illinois, the disc was the tool to use in that sandy soil. The rains wash through the sand much differently from the way they do in our clay soils. On my fields here, a disc will level the ground better than other tools, but rock hard clods form out of the clay after it rains. If I've used a moldboard plow, I'd rather level it with a spike-tooth harrow. This is also called a "section harrow," with six rows of eight inch spikes on it, like a big, four foot square rake. When I've chisel-plowed the ground, and the land is still rough with growing plants in it, a spring-tooth harrow is the tool for the job. It has curved teeth like a cultivator and digs in the ground, lifting the clods and chunks up with a springing motion. I've heard of another harrow called a chain-link harrow for spreading cowpies around in the pasture, which is a great idea. Spreading the manure out and aerating the ground at the same time is beneficial for pasture land.

Someone also told me about a spring-tooth harrow that has smaller springs than mine, the size of cultivator tines. I'd be interested in learning more about any old horse-drawn harrows and would like to buy some parts, as mine are pretty worn out. A "wheater" is a funny looking harrow that you pull through the wheat fields this time of year to scratch the surface, breaking up the crust but not disturbing the wheat. Harrowing is used when a shallow tillage is all you need, like preparing a seed bed or covering up freshly sown seed.

One of the most useful jobs for my spike-tooth harrow (or a rake in my smaller garden) is to run over the rows a week after I've planted but before the plants are up. This gets thousands of germinating weeds but doesn't bother the big seeds like squash, beans, corn or potatoes. It has been three weeks since we planted potatoes, and from a distance, two different people informed me that no weeds were growing there. That's what it looked like to me, but when I got down on my hands and knees and examined closely, I saw a small green weed about every square inch. So I dragged the field with the spike-tooth harrow and eliminated a huge amount of hand hoeing I would have had to do otherwise. Once the potatoes come up, I can only cultivate between the rows with the tractor. The weeds in the row will require the hoe. Now, the potatoes will have a chance to get up, shade out the weeds in the row, and keep the hoeing to a minimum, I hope. But it was a bit harrowing driving through the soon-to-be sprouting spuds.

April 18, 1995

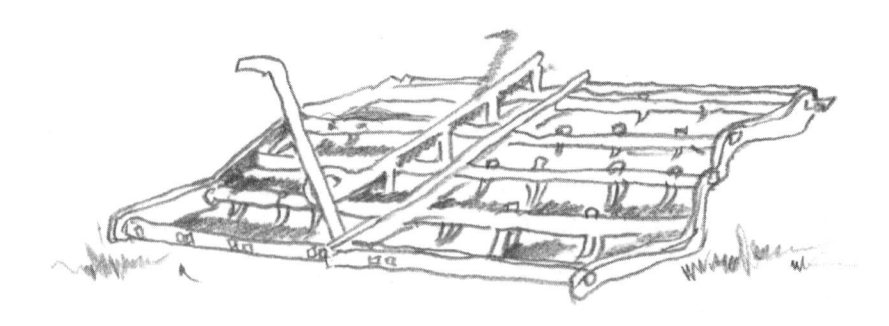

Asparagus and Rhubarb

Two of our earliest crops, asparagus and rhubarb, are old-timers' favorites, ready to harvest now in early spring. They are perennials, which means they come back every year without having to replant them. An asparagus bed is set in the spring by planting roots, preferably two-year-old ones. We got ours, the Mary Washington variety, at a nursery in McMinnville, TN.

Asparagus plants are either male or female. Males are bigger on the average and have the advantage of not going to seed, thus the plants don't spread where you don't want them to. This has not been a problem for us. What was a problem was following the instructions about digging a foot-deep trench, planting the roots, and gradually filling the trench as the plants come up. It was a huge amount of work, and at a foot deep, the plants were suffocating in a heavy clay subsoil.

After two patches that were failures, I plowed a five inch furrow, added some compost, set the roots about 18 inches apart, and raked some good soil over the top of them. The roots, now only four to five inches deep, grew well, and we've had lovely green spears of asparagus every spring since then. The deep planting method must be for a rich, sandy soil like they have in the Midwest, but around here, asparagus needs to be closer to the surface. I try to keep the patch mowed or mulched in early spring so the young shoots are easy to harvest, cutting them at ground level when they are 6 to 12 inches tall. After a month or so, we just let the whole patch grow up.

Asparagus is a beautiful fern-like plant with feathery leaves and a pretty color, a nice addition to the garden landscape. I mow the patch down in late summer, spread compost, and can harvest a few more spears before the fall frost puts them to sleep. We like asparagus raw or lightly steamed. It is so good to have a delicious green vegetable in mid-April while we wait patiently for the spinach and lettuce to get big enough to eat.

The other early spring crop we love is rhubarb, locally called "pie plant." It divides easily, and we have helped others get a patch of it going just by digging a side shoot off a mother plant from our patch.

We have the green variety, which is quite prolific and tastes great, though it is mighty sour. I'd like to try a red variety and see if there is much difference. The green pies we make don't look nearly as good as they taste.

The plants are set about two to three feet apart and given a liberal dose of compost in the spring. Keep them free of weeds the first year and next spring you can start harvesting the stalks. Rhubarb leaves are toxic, so eat only the stalks. Prune off the round stalk that is sending up a flower and seed head so that the plant can put its energy into growing the leaves with their delicious stems. Both rhubarb and asparagus can be mulched to retain moisture and to keep the weeds down. I usually cut the leaves of the rhubarb off the stalks right away and leave them to mulch the plant.

Rhubarb is probably classified as a vegetable, but the pies taste like fruit. We simply steam or boil the stalks and then mash them up with some honey to make good pie filling. Tapioca or another thickener can be added if it's too runny. It's best with a cup or two of berries added to make a fantastic berry-rhubarb pie, and it's much easier to harvest than the berries.

April 19, 1994

Wildflower Hike

Just as fruits, vegetables and grains feed our bodies, the world of flowers feeds our souls. The beautiful colors of blooming plants throughout the year gives universal and indescribable good feelings to the beholder. Many of our native wildflowers are also pretty in the garden. Daisies and black-eyed susans are common, but never boring. The wild white yarrow, a good medicine for urinary infections, comes in garden varieties of red and yellow. Phlox, whose purple blooms dot the woodlands around here, has many other colors to choose from for sparkling up banks as a ground cover.

The wild iris, or blue flag, is found down by the creek, where you'll find jewelweed, also called touch-me-not because the seed capsule springs open when you touch it. We let jewelweed grow up around our cabin, so we can watch the hummingbirds gather the nectar, and we like to have it handy for squeezing its healing stem juice on a poison ivy rash. A spring walk in the woods will wear out your wildflower identification book, and you'll just revel in the red and white trilliums, mayapples, columbine, and the hundred more tiny, beautiful gems without caring who's who.

Massive carpets of fringed phacelia, bluets, and spring beauties beneath our feet and blooming buckeyes and locust overhead create a flower tunnel. The old favorites - dandelions and violets - sprinkle color everywhere, and deep in the woods you'll find the deep purple larkspur. Jack-in-the-pulpit has an interesting striped hood over the pistil part of the flower, but don't let anyone trick you into eating this Indian turnip, it's hot! Shooting stars, hepatica and foam flower adorn the cliffs; wood betony and gentians, the damp spots. The wild sedum is the wild relative of the fat-leafed live forever. In the meadow, buttercups and daisies are out, and late summer will host a whole new array of flowers; St. John's wort, goldenrod, iron weed and asters.

Back in the garden, our bleeding hearts are really heart-shaped and dripping, and the chamomile blossoms are almost ready to harvest. Brilliant iridescent purples come from the verbena and old-fashioned rose campion. Rosa rugosas have opened lovely red blossoms which will later turn into large red rose hips. The pink cabbage rose is flowering, and the miniature shrub roses are loaded with buds. The rose family includes many flowering fruit plants, too, with their five-petaled blossoms that adorn the landscape, such as apples, pears, and the lovely blackberries brightening our hillsides now. I love blackberry blooms in May and the berries in July, but you can have their thorns the rest of the year.

Marigolds are beneficial in the vegetable garden where there are other attractive flowers, like the hibiscus-flowered okra and the colorful bean blossoms. Along with big yellow squash flowers, we'll have beautiful wild morning glories, akin to the night-blooming moonflower vine we grow on the barn wall, poisonous jimson weed, the ever-present heal-all, pink smartweed, plus galinsoga, whose lovely white flowers don't look so lovely smothering out my veggies.

At this point, my soul is full, I've got the hoe out, and I'm getting hungry!

May 23, 1995

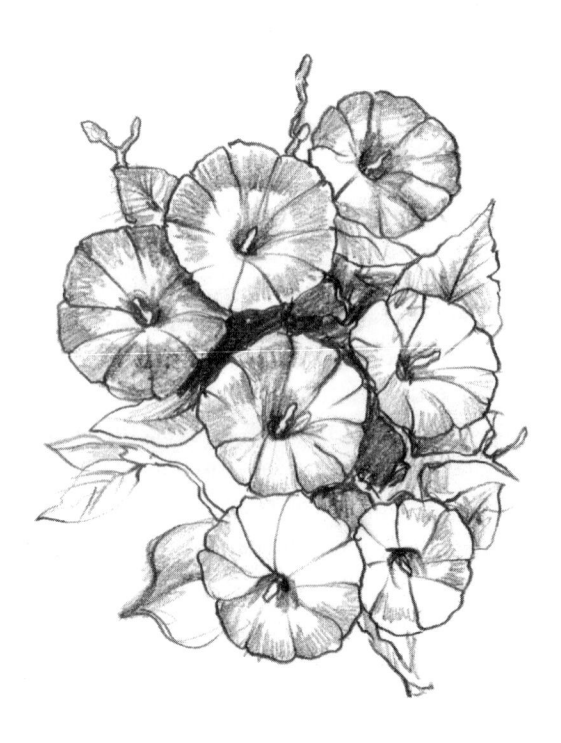

Hoeing

Hoe, hoe, hoe. There are many reasons to hoe, almost as many as we can think of to put it off. Delaying your cultivation is a mistake, though. The weeds will take advantage of the situation. I like to hoe around my seedlings as soon as they pop up, lightly tickling the ground nearby without getting too close, as that might disturb them.

Weeds are Mother Nature's way of covering the bare ground. Their persistence and presence show the truth that "nature abhors a vacuum." Our introduced plants don't have a chance with the powerful growth forces inherent in weeds. It is this phenomenon that we can learn from. As the bare ground draws in plant growth, we can choose what grows there. As we hoe the weeds out, our plants have a good opportunity to fill in that bare ground. The nice loose soil packs after a hard spring rain and a few days later this crust needs to be broken up. Just because you don't see weeds doesn't mean you should wait to hoe. As soon as a fistful of soil falls apart when it's dropped, it's time to hoe.

A wide, flat hoe can be dragged along the side of the row, killing all the invisible but germinating weed seeds and bringing air into the ground. Where the dirt falls off the hoe and onto the ground it will smother some weeds, and the ones that do come through will be weakened. Short, chopping strokes are necessary where the soil is hard. If you let the weeds grow and then go out to hoe, you have to pull each weed first, shake the dirt off, and then hoe around the plants. This is much more time-consuming and inevitably happens in a few of my fields, and then it seems like more work than the crop is worth.

Hoeing also checks evaporation, which means that the capillary action of soil moisture wicking out into the atmosphere is prevented when the crust is broken. Plants love loose soil around them. As the plants get bigger, I heap up dirt around them, again as part of weed control, to hold in the moisture and to help keep the plants from falling over. Corn, beans, potatoes and tomatoes all like to be hilled. The bigger your hoe is, the easier this job is. I don't hill up plants like lettuce, cabbage, carrots or onions.

Sweet potatoes are planted on a hill. When they are young, the hoeing moves the dirt away from the plant, and subsequent tillage, when the plants are bigger, brings the dirt back up against the plant. This principle applies to most crops that get hilled, as the dirt is at first moved away, then later raked back in. Again, this only works before the weeds are present. Otherwise, you have to pull up the weeds totally or else they'll re-sprout.

Another important aspect of hoeing is to be present and observing your crop. We control bean and potato beetles while hoeing by squashing them and checking for eggs under the leaves. I carry seeds of the various plants I'm hoeing, so I can slip them in the row if there's a weak stand. Early signs of disease or deficiencies can be spotted and dealt with when hoeing. Manure tea, made by soaking manure in water for a few days, will perk up some yellowing, weak plants.

Hoeing also teaches you about body posture. The way you hold the hoe and your back while working greatly determines how you'll feel later on. I try to switch hands and sides so that I use all of my body, and to do as much as I can standing straight up, although it is mostly backbreaking work however you do it.

The nitrogen withheld in the soil's organic matter is released with hoeing, as many small forms of life are killed and their bodies consequently supply nitrogen as they decay. Hoeing thus helps to fertilize our plants. People have been hoeing since the dawn of civilization, and no doubt it is ingrained in our human psyche. The ritual of getting out there and enthusiastically working the soil, chopping weeds and tending our gardens is important for ourselves as well as for our plants.

June 13, 1995

CHAPTER III

Summer Bounty

Tomatoes	63
Peppers	66
Sweet Corn	68
Green Beans	71
Melons	73
Cucumbers	75
Butternuts	77
Sweet Potatoes	80
Hilling	83
Flowers	85
Weeds	87

"I was determined to know beans."

Thoreau

Tomatoes

Tomatoes are many people's favorite garden vegetable. Even folks who don't grow a garden may set out a few 'mater plants, because nothing tastes as good as a homegrown one. The two things money can't buy are love and homegrown tomatoes.

We start seed indoors about the middle of March, but if you want extra early tomatoes you can start some Early Girls in February. Keep them warm in a sunny location and transplant them into bigger pots as they grow. Tomatoes are extremely frost tender, so wait until after the last frost before you set them out. When is the last frost? This year it was in mid-April, around our average frost-free date of April 20. But I've seen it as early as March 28 or as late as the killer frost of '97 on May 16, which got many tomato plants, including 400 of ours.

We usually sprout the seeds in trays with a mixture of equal parts sand, soil and compost. When they get their first true leaves, we line them out in the bottom of the cold frame, which has a three inch deep bed of the same mixture in it, at two inch centers. Moistened before we transplant them to the garden, a knife checkerboards the rows, and they are lifted out plant by plant with a little soil still around their roots.

Unlike most crops, tomatoes (and their cousin, tobacco) like to grow on the same spot every year. They like a compost made of their own stalks and a slightly raw compost poor in nitrogen. Too much nitrogen will give you big leafy plants but not much fruit. Disease is a problem in the tomato patch, and planting time is the time to combat it. Give your plants plenty of space, at least three feet apart in rows four to five feet apart. You'll get more and better tomatoes from less plants.

Celebrity is still our main crop for selling, but I also like Parks Whopper. Both are extremely disease resistant and make delicious, big fruits all season long. For our own table, we grow heirloom varieties with supreme flavor and slurpy juiciness. Bradley is tops around here for a pink tomato, and many of our customers want them, too. But a Bradley is hard to ship. They are so soft and juicy that they bruise easily. Brandywine is an old-fashioned German pink tomato that everyone enjoys. We are trying a yellow Brandywine this year to see what they're like. Lyman Hawkins gave me the Oxheart, and it is now a staple here – huge, pointed, meaty, pink tomatoes on a much more delicate plant than a Brandywine, which has big, fat leaves. All of these heirlooms are easy to save seed from. Just let a few ripe tomatoes rot two days in a bucket, then rinse and dry the seeds.

For paste tomatoes, we like the old-fashioned Roma, although we've tried many others. I'm trying Amish paste tomatoes this year in the never-ending search for the perfect canning tomato. Cherry tomatoes come back in the same place every year and are handy to have near the kitchen doorstep. You never know when a summer salad will need a tomato perk-me-up, and you can step out your door and remedy the situation.

A few insects, like stinkbugs, mar the fruit, but do not do appreciable damage. The tomato hornworm is always covered with white parasites on the back, and the few that live to make a cocoon turn into such beautiful sphinx moths, I'll let them do it. Diseases are a problem in the gardens of many people, but we have been lucky so far. By not using chemical fertilizers we don't force the plants to grow too fast and we give them lots of space. I usually mist them with a horsetail tea in the summer. It has a high silica content and a drying effect on the plants.

After planting and hilling them up a bit, the tomatoes are soon knee high and ready for cages. I'm a firm believer in caging the sprawling buggers, as tomatoes are not climbers and have no tendrils. All forms of pruning, staking and tying them up pale in comparison to tomato cages. I get 39" woven wire with the holes big enough for a good sized 'mater to go through, and cut it in sections about six or seven feet long. Then I tie the ends together to make a two-foot diameter cylinder and slip it over a two-foot wide tomato plant. If you put them on too early, the tomato just grows through the holes and back down on the ground. You want to bend the branches inward a bit and put the cage over them, so they'll grow upward and sprawl out the top. A tobacco stake woven through the cage and driven into the ground will keep everything upright.

After caging, we mulch the whole patch with old hay. A 5x5 roll mulches a four foot wide strip about 150 feet long. Hay mown with a disc mower is more cut up and hence easier to unroll than sicklebar-cut hay. A big round bale is brought to the end of the row, and we tear off each side with a pitchfork until we get the inside tootsie roll down to a size where we can push it off. Long, wide layers of hay are left to be spread on the field about a foot thick. We carry the inner roll to the inner part of the patch and continue tearing and mulching. Then we go swimming.

The rest is harvest. For market, a green tomato is picked when it gets its first blush of red. "Vine-ripe tomatoes" are a joke in the produce trade. A vine-ripe tomato is juice after shipping, so they are all picked green and ripened at the store. But you, the home gardener, have the best thing money can't buy, or at least the second best.

June 8, 1999

Peppers

Peppers like it hot and dry, so they are really happy now. As other plants are wilting, peppers are getting greener. We can help simulate their natural habitat, which must be a desert, by keeping the ground weed-free and unmulched. Tomatoes and potatoes, their cousins in the nightshade family, enjoy a good mulch of hay, but I think peppers would rather have hot, bare ground.

Peppers need full sun. Last year we planted our patch in rich bottom land, but it got afternoon shade. The plants grew tall and thin, and our yield was low. This year on top of the hill, they are shorter, stockier, and full of fat fruit. We start the seeds indoors in March, and they get special treatment. Peppers need extra warmth to germinate, so we either put a piece of glass over the tray to create a greenhouse effect, or set them on a shelf close to our wood stove to stay warm. When they get their first true leaves, we pot them up in a mixture of soil, sand and compost.

When all danger of frost is past, they are big enough to go out in the garden. Here they grow slowly at first. Tomatoes double in size every few days, while the peppers just sit there and wait for summer. They are set two feet apart in rows three and a half feet apart, and they need frequent cultivation when young. Eventually they fill up the row, and are now the healthiest plants in the garden (except for the weeds). Although they need fertilizer, too much available nitrogen will lessen the yield. Good garden soil with a little compost is all you need for good peppers. Insects don't bother peppers much. We get a few stem borers early on, and every now and then a worm in the fruit, but that's to be expected.

Our favorite variety is Golden Summer, a light green pepper that turns a bright, golden color and has thick, juicy flesh with lots of flavor. Adriane is an orange one that's also delicious. King of the North and California Wonder are the standard dark green peppers which turn a beautiful red when ripe. We have a purple pepper this year that's gorgeous, but just so-so on flavor and texture. Bell peppers can be sliced in half-inch strips, dried, and then used as a nice addition to wintertime soups. Peppers can be pickled, too, as we recall from Peter

Piper's tongue-twisting experience with pickling a peck of them.

Italian Bull Horns are zesty chili peppers I really enjoy. The Hungarian Wax are banana peppers with a hint of something more than a cold, sweet pepper flavor. They are long and yellow and turn bright red. The hot banana peppers look just like them, but you sure can taste the difference. But it's the jalapenos and cayennes that separate the strong from the wimps, and I guess I'm a wimp, 'cause every time I eat a raw or pickled hot pepper I immediately get the hiccups. Habeneros are even hotter and more flavorful, but the hottest are the little-bitty African and Thai peppers that can set fire to your mouth. Have a fire extinguisher handy, or at least a big glass of water. Cayennes are the most medicinal of the peppers. Oddly enough, they are recommended for peptic ulcers. They also keep colds away, clean out excess mucus, and are great for your circulation. We dry them to crush up and make a powder. A word of warning, though, wash your hands after cutting them up and before you scratch your eye or take a leak.

In salsa, stuffed, sauteed or steamed, peppers are a great summertime food. But I believe they are best eaten raw when they are ripe; a sweet, juicy fruit from a dry dusty garden.

August 8, 1995

Sweet Corn

Fresh sweet corn is summer at its best. Fresh means mom puts on the pot of water to boil as dad heads to the corn patch, so the time between picking and dropping in the boiling water is a matter of minutes. Corn on the cob is a meal in itself. Try it raw for a delicious treat instead of a salad. It's a great main course with starch and protein, and as a sweet dessert it can't be beat. I've never been able to top Uncle Frank's 15 ears at one setting, but I can pass the rest of dinner up and eat close to half that.

Probably no plant is more important in American agriculture today than corn. The sheer amount of plant matter it produces is tremendous, as it turns an almost two-dimensional field into three dimensions with its six foot or taller stalks. The insect energy is intense in our fields, with constant buzzing and flittering. Sweet corn is easy to grow in your garden if you have ample space and compost. It is a heavy feeder and loves full sun. We start planting it in mid-April - when the oak leaves are as big as squirrels' ears - and continue planting new patches every few weeks until the first of July. We were eating our first planting of Early Sunglow, a small, 65 day variety, before we planted our last patch this year. By planting varieties with different maturity dates, you can have a continuous supply of fresh corn.

Funk's G-90 is our favorite, a bi-color that's always fabulous. It's at its best raw or boiled for two minutes, but doesn't can well. For the 55 minutes in the pressure canner that corn requires, Golden Queen is a better canning variety. It is the yellow sister of Tennessee's all-time favorite white, Silver Queen. There are many kinds of sweet corn, all of them good. The first plantings of corn are sown thickly, about four kernels per foot, so there is "one for the bugs, one for the crow, one to rot, and one to grow." If they come up too thickly, the first hoeing takes out the excess. Later plantings at a foot apart, their preferred spacing, do fine, though I like to plant twice as many and then thin them to be sure I get a good stand.

Crows are a real problem. They walk down the row just after the corn has sprouted, digging up the seedlings for the kernel. Years ago I

Chapter 3 Summer Bounty

soaked the seed in cayenne pepper and that kept them off of it, until they got a liking for Mexican food. From an old-time farming book, I got the idea of a little pine tar mixed in the seed, and this works great. After stirring a tablespoon into a pound of seed, I add a little dry dirt or rock powder so it's easier to handle. Another helpful method is to put out some field corn in piles along the patch as an offering. The crows will eat it first, and your sweet corn will get too big for them to bother. Nothing much else eats the corn plants, unless your cows get out. Cultivate frequently and hill them up on the last pass. You can throw out some buckwheat or soybean seed now and grow a cover crop between the rows of corn. Pole beans and pumpkins will produce in a corn patch, but can take it over, too.

I use the word "patch" often when talking about corn because it is wind pollinated and consequently doesn't make full ears when planted in a single row. I like big blocks of corn, and use it as a first year crop on new land, as its towering growth shades out the grass and perennial weeds. Corn needs no sprays whatsoever. The earworm in the tip tells you your corn is sweet and organic. Don't worry about the Japanese beetles in the silk, their presence often draws birds who'll also eat the earworm. When the silk turns brown and the ears feel plump, the corn is ripe. To freeze corn, blanch the shucked ears for four minutes, then quickly cool by immersing in cold water. Cut off the kernels and fill up your baggies. Seven half-bushel baskets from the garden put about 25 quarts in the freezer.

A favorite way to eat corn is roasted on the open fire. Rake the coals from a summer bonfire into a nice bed, and put a grate on a few rocks about three or four inches above them. Place freshly harvested ears on the grate, and turn them every few minutes until the husk turns light brown, about 15 minutes. You can dip them in spring water beforehand and they'll steam, but I like the roasted flavor when they aren't dipped. Any way you do it, you are making for a real summer party. Hickory King makes great roastin' ears.

After harvest, work the stalks in the ground, or haul them to the compost pile where they can be layered with manure. I often follow an early corn patch with the garlic crop, which is planted in September. The garlic gets another heavy feeding of compost and a couple of hay mulchings. The land gets really fertile, and I can follow the garlic, which gets pulled next year in late June, with the last corn planting. Some of our sweet corn got overripe, so we let it dry and harvested it for our new chicks. They are doing great on it, along with kitchen scraps, and now at eight weeks old, are about half grown. Pigs can be turned into the old corn patch to eat it and work it back into the ground. Cattle love the stalks as well as the ears, and horses are tamed by this magical plant. Although corn prices are the same as they were 100 years ago, wrecking havoc in rural America, this native grain continues to be the backbone of our agriculture and economy. And it never tasted better than the one I just ate.

August 10, 1999

Green Beans

You can can beans. Green beans are one of the most canned of the garden vegetables. Rows of bright green beans in jars enliven the pantry shelf and insure good eating next winter. As usual, we start with lots of compost worked into the garden beds. Beans also appreciate lime, wood ashes, or both, sprinkled on the ground a few months before planting time, which is about May 1st. A frost will kill beans, so hold your horses when spring planting fever hits. A May 1st planting will usually catch up to an April 20 planting anyway.

Rich soil is important for a healthy green bean crop. A slow-growing bean patch will likely be bean beetle food. Beans sprout fast, and a row of their heart-shaped leaves looks rather cute. A quick cultivation is a good idea as soon as they get their first true leaves. A few weeks later, they like another cultivation and hilling up. Pulling the loosened soil up to the stalks helps support them and keeps plenty of moisture available.

To beat the beetles, I like the quick maturing varieties of green beans. Any 55 to 65 day variety will make beans by early July, before the yellow beetle larvae lace the plants. A Mexican bean beetle looks like a big brown ladybug, and lays masses of yellow eggs on the undersides of the leaves. Periodic checking and squashing bugs in the bean patch is a good idea. You aren't supposed to pick or work in the bean patch while it's wet because that spreads disease. On the other hand, letting mature beans touch wet ground causes rot. We all loved the three inches of late June rain, though we eventually had to get in there and pick the green beans while the ground was a little damper than I like.

Romano is an Italian, flat-podded green bean I really enjoy. This year we're trying an old heirloom called Bountiful that is also a flat-podded one and is living up to its name by producing bountiful yields. Royal Burgundy is a pretty, purple bean with a purple flower and stalks, too. When you pour boiling water on them, they turn green, but the water does not change color. Where does the purple go? Blue Lake is another good old standard for round green beans. Varieties I'm not crazy about are Provider and Contender, newer ones that lack the old-time beany flavor. Missouri Wonder and Kentucky Wonder are delicious pole beans, often staked with the native bamboo river cane. Half-runners are popular around here, and can be staked with short branches or left just to sprawl. I've planted a local short-cut bean called Hixie from the Haysville Community. It's a green bean with swelled-up shelly beans inside it. We're also saving seed from an old purple, flat bean that's been locally grown for years, and we always grow October shelly beans.

On the porch, snappin' and chattin', we prepare a few bushels while the wood cookstove gets fired up and the water is put on to boil. This job is much faster with the stringless green beans. Quart jars are washed and scalded, then filled with washed beans. Green beans can be packed raw or slightly cooked. The only advantage I see to heating them before packing is less time in the pressure canner before it reaches 240°. A little salt can be added to each jar, but is not necessary.

The pressure cooker is necessary for canning low-acid foods like green beans. We pour boiling water over the packed jars of beans to one-half inch below the rim. The jars are then wiped off, and new lids, which have been setting in hot water, are screwed on top. The jars are set in the canner, the lid tightened, and the fire stoked. When steam comes whistling out, the valve is closed, and we look at the clock when the pressure reaches 10 pounds. We keep it at 10 pounds pressure for 25 minutes, then prepare the next batch of seven jars while we wait for the pressure to go back down. They are set on a towel, and soon we hear the reassuring ping of the vacuum causing the lids to seal. It's as easy as beans, and anyone can can.

A favorite way to eat them is to saute onions, garlic, and a cayenne pepper for a couple of minutes, then add a quart of green beans and a pint of pintos from the cellar shelf. Season with cumin, salt and oregano and serve with cornbread.

July 6, 1999

Melons

Melons are traditionally "hill" crops. Why do they get this special treatment? These warmth-loving vegetables have deep taproots that dive down for soil moisture. Thus they are able to withstand dry weather. The small hills we make for them dry out and simulate the desert conditions these crops originated in.

As organic farmers, we have another reason for hilling up the melons. They are heavy feeders and require high soil fertility. So each hill gets to sit on a bucketful of rotted manure. Muskmelons are planted in hills about four or five feet apart and watermelons about six to eight feet apart. Dig a hole and fill it with the rotted manure. Then rake good topsoil over it to make a hill about two feet in diameter. Into this hill, I usually add compost, and this year I threw in a shovelful of sand. I got this idea from one of my old farming books. It rang true when I thought of the desert that brought us these great desserts.

I like to get the first crop of weeds by harrowing the field once or twice before I plant the seeds, which is about the second week of May. Six to eight seeds are planted in a six inch circle in the center of the hill. Loose soil, with the sand or something else to keep it from packing, is lightly pressed about an inch over the seeds. Loose soil is very important for the quick sprouting and growing of the tender young plants. It's at this stage that Mother Nature sends in one of her most strict house cleaners, the flea beetle.

I believe that insect pests are nature's way of restoring organic matter to the soil. If your garden is not humus-rich, fluffy, and full of organic matter, Mother Nature will help you by sending in bugs to turn whatever is growing there back in to the soil. (Thanks a lot, Mom!) A covering of plant bed cloth (also called a floating row cover, or Remay) will keep the bugs off while the plants get a head start. We sure don't recommend poison, though, because poisons kill off many of the beneficial insects that are out there. (Poisons may not be good for you, either.)

Once the plants get a little size on them, I thin them to three per hill and they take off and grow well.

A muskmelon can rot if it sits on the ground, so I may mulch between the hills. But I don't do that until after the ground gets thoroughly warmed, maybe by the beginning of July. Bees pollinate the flowers and the melons start to form. Right before the melons are ripe, some of the plants wilt and die. This can be from a borer on the root, which can be extracted and the plant saved if it's done early enough. It could also be one of the many diseases melons are prone to. Powdery mildew and fusarium wilt are common ones. I just suffer through losing a few plants, pulling them and removing them from the garden. The vines that are left usually make more melons that we can eat, anyway.

We've been saving a good cantaloupe from seed Faye Kirby gave me. Hales Best Jumbo is a standard favorite, and Little Jenny Linds have finally given us good honeydew melons. Rattlesnake is my favorite watermelon. In good years, we have hundreds of them, many over fifty pounds. Other years haven't been so successful. Charleston Grey, Crimson Sweet, and Amish Moon and Stars are other favorites of mine. With watermelon rows eight feet apart, rows of beans can be grown in between and harvested just as the melon vines reach them.

There is a saying about melons: "eat alone or leave alone". We like to gorge on them without other food to interfere with their digestion. Mother Nature is a sweet mom (what smells better than a ripe muskmelon that slips from the stem when you pick it up?) if only we follow her rules and guidance.

June 18, 1996

Cucumbers

 I awoke from my slumbers to find numbers of cucumbers packed in jars still filled with dill. But of course, the story started long before. Cukes, as we affectionately call them, are closely related to cantaloupes. The leaves have that same prickly nature and, as in all plant relatives, the flowers are similar. I've heard old-time gardeners say you should not plant them next to each other, because the cantaloupes won't be as sweet, but I've never tried it, so I can't verify this. I do know they love compost and need to get off to a good start. Being frost tender, we wait until May to get the pickle patch planted. We usually just grow one variety of pickling cukes, Miss Pickler. They taste fine as a salad cuke and, as the name implies, make great pickles. Marketmore and Straight Eight are the salad cukes I grow to sell. There are white cucumbers and many other varieties, including Asian yard-long ones, but we keep the pickle patch pretty simple.

 Just as we have squash bugs, potato beetles, and bean beetles, sure enough there is a cucumber beetle. Actually there are two; a green spotted one, and a black and white striped one, both small and quick. The most damage they do is through spreading disease, and healthy plants resist them well. A row cover over the young plants will protect them through the tender stage, but it needs to be removed when they start flowering so the bees can do their job.

 Gardening on a large scale has found me making rows and not hills for many of the cucurbits. They grow just fine in a big, long row, and this year we used this to our advantage. Good compost got the cucumbers up and growing, and after thinning to about eight inches apart, they started vining. The nearby beans and zucchini were looking worried, as you would be with a row of running vines four feet away heading toward you. This garden plot was small and tight, and I had planted things a little too close.

 A cucumber tendril gave me the idea of putting up a cuke fence, something I couldn't have easily done if we'd grown them in the traditional hills. Seven cattle panels were tied to metal posts which had been driven into the rows at eight feet intervals, making a long, vertical cuke patch. But cucumbers are not pole beans, and even with a little encouragement by tucking them in, they were still heading over to the bean row. Years of growing in hills and running on the ground had dulled their innate sense of climbing, although each plant had one or two branches that were feeling their way up the trellis.

Cukes are great hiders, and both Jed and Mary walked by them without finding one to eat. Ryan, age five and closer to the ground, spotted some, and he and I picked six pecks from the patch, much to everyone else's surprise. Time to pickle! A grape leaf goes in the bottom of each jar. Mom did this because grape leaves have natural alum, which helps keep the pickles crisp. A half a dozen or more garlic cloves are dropped in, and these are delicacies in themselves, as pickled garlic. Then the small cucumbers are packed in whole and the larger ones quartered. A couple sprigs of dill, a bay leaf, and a teaspoon of allspice are added, and then the jar is filled up with a near-boiling solution of brine.

The brine is made with a gallon each of apple cider vinegar and water, with two cups of salt, and is more than enough for 14 quarts. The jars are put into a water-bath canner and boiled for 15 minutes, then removed. Soon you'll hear the ping of the lid sealing and know that in a few months you'll have your pickles. But who can wait? The extra brine is used to soak other cukes, garlic, and dill in a bowl; and lo and behold, they disappear after a few days. There are many other pickle recipes, and I hope the Chronicle gets a few readers to send theirs in.

Back in the garden, I make a decision to teach these cucumber vines a lesson. If you climb the fence, you're fine. But the branches wrapping around the green beans are getting too friendly, so a whack with the machete prunes them off. The beans are saved and the pickle patch is not hurt a bit, just trained to go up and not out.

Try a cucumber sandwich or cold cucumber soup. They are also delicious fresh from the garden with (or without) salt and pepper. Put them in a crock for old-fashioned brine pickles. One wonders at the numbers of ways to enjoy cucumbers.

June 29, 1999

Butternuts

Butternut squash are the perfect crop; easy to grow, easy to store, and easy to eat. I have learned how to raise them so that they are easy on the land, too. The half-acre garden where the beans and sweet potatoes grew last year was sown in rye and Austrian peas for the winter cover crop. In mid-April, I ran the bush hog through the foot tall plants in strips, leaving a four foot strip unmown. Then I spread composted manure in the mown strips.

I love my new tractor. It has really low gears so I can pull the manure spreader of compost slowly, so most of the compost is dropped right behind the spreader. Next, I worked the compost into the ground in the four foot wide strips, so the centers of these strips were about eight feet apart. I used a double-digging spading machine for plowing these beds. Butternuts are a strongly vining plant and like to be planted with eight feet between the rows. Then I let the field rest until early May, so the plowed land could digest and readjust. The strips with the cover crops kept growing.

I put the subsoiler on the small Ford (the tractor Dad used to call the big Ford), and ran it two feet deep in the centers of the beds, leaving a perfect furrow on the top. The breaking up of the hardpan allows the deep tap roots of the squash to penetrate into the subsoil.

Whenever we ate a butternut last winter, we saved the seeds. They slip easily from the bright orange pulp after you split a squash in half prior to baking, and are dried on a plate in a sunny window before being stored in a glass jar. I grabbed the jar and poured some of the precious seeds into my right hand and gently rubbed them as I walked down the row, dropping them one by one into the furrow. I love sowing seed by hand. Rubbing them helps to unstick them, as they tend to stick together. I aim for one every six inches or so. But my back was a little sore from yesterday's corn patch, so I didn't bend over but dropped them from waist level. I'm not too fussy with squash seed, because they will be thinned later to 18 inches apart, and I have plenty of seed.

After sowing, I do the duck-waddle back over the row, dragging my feet through the dirt covering the furrow. The rye and peas beside me are now knee-high and full of activity. Insects buzz around, and the roots are busy structuring the soil. Nearby strawberries are still blooming and promising sweet rewards in a few weeks when I'll be hoeing the squash.

Many squash varieties cross-pollinate with each other, so you can't reliably save the seed, but butternuts only cross with two other varieties, as far as I know. One is the Tahitian melon-squash, which is huge, and for a while I had very large butternuts resulting from such a cross. We called them world-feeders. They tasted great and grew well, but it was hard to sell a five or ten pound squash with green splotches on it. So I bought new seed a few years ago and am keeping it pure by not growing the Tahitian melon squash.

Squash sprouts rapidly in warm ground, and soon our rows will be full of pretty plants, and pretty weeds, too. But the extra seed I sowed will make extra squash plants, and their big leaves will shade out a lot of foxtail, pigweed, ragweed and other obnoxious weeds until they are thinned. An easy swipe of the hoe will wipe out the extras, where the weeds require you to reach down, pull them up, shake the dirt off, burn them in a ritual and dance the hokey-pokey over their ashes. (Just kidding on those last two.) In other words, a weed is a plant out of place, and I'd rather hoe squash plants than the weeds. After a few cultivations, the squash start running. By now the rye and peas are blooming and are five or six feet tall, with wonderful soil building going on underground and vibrant energy above. The sharp rye leaves point skyward, drawing in silica energy, and the soft pea leaves unfold horizontally and warmly invite calcium energy to activity. It almost seems a shame to mow it down, but that's what I do. Conveniently, the rye and peas are now a mulch for the squash, without me having to haul it in from somewhere else.

The butternut vines soon fill in the whole field, then flower and make their tan, pear-shaped fruits. Persistent pigweeds raise their heads above the sea of squash leaves, only to be whacked off by Sinbad the Sailor and his mighty machete. By late August, the troops come in with baskets and pruning shears to clip and collect the bounty. Butternuts will keep all winter long on a pantry shelf if the stem is not broken off of the fruit, which is why we cut them with the shears. A damp rag wipes off the spot of dirt where they rested on the earth, and they are ready for market. Stick a butternut in the oven for an hour and pull out a soft, custard-like pudding of a dessert that's sweet, delicious, and really good for you. The orange flesh indicates it's high in Vitamin A, and it is a prized food for both its taste and nutrition.

It's easy to cook, tastes good, stores for a year, and the field where we grew it is now more fertile than before with no input besides a few loads of compost and some hoeing. Perfect!

Butternut squash pie

Bake a butternut until soft. Scoop out flesh and mash with a fork. Beat 3 eggs and add a cup of milk, 1/4 cup of honey, a pinch of cinnamon and nutmeg. Vanilla, allspice, cloves and/or ginger can also spice up this "pumpkin" pie.

Three tablespoons of fresh butter is cut into 2 cups of our whole wheat flour with a fork and then our fingers, then enough water or buttermilk is added to make a rollable dough. This is quickly rolled out and put into one big or two small pie pans. All of the other ingredients are beat together well and then poured in the pie shell and baked with a big hickory or oak fire (350 degrees, I suppose) for 45 minutes or until a knife inserted comes out clean.

Serve with fresh whipped cream.

May 11, 1999

Sweet Potatoes

Bedding down the sweet potatoes is a late March ritual we do soon after the spring equinox. Now that each day has more sun than not, all of the heat-loving summer plants start stirring. They may not perk up their heads like the pretty spring wildflowers, but seeds and roots alike know it's time to think about growing again. An old cold frame, or a bank on a southern slope, will make a good sweet potato bed. Traditionally, a layer of horse manure goes in first. When moistened, it heats up, giving the bed some bottom warmth. Sand, with a little compost added, is shoveled on top of this about two inches deep, and then we're ready for the roots.

Sweet potatoes are a long-season tropical plant in the morning glory family. They are an important food worldwide, and many cultures live on them. The yam, a name often applied to the red varieties, is actually a different family of viny, starchy root crops grown in Africa and South America. Sometimes late in the season, we'll find a few flowers on the sweet potato vines, and they'll have the twisty, trumpet shape typical of the morning glory family.

We don't get sweet potato seed, we propagate them from their roots. A fun thing to do is to put a sweet potato in a jar of water, held part of the way out by toothpicks inserted in the potato's sides. With the eyes up and the root in the water, vines will soon be growing all over your kitchen windowsill. This is a quick way to have a beautiful houseplant, and the vines can be pulled off and planted in the garden. The sweet potato plant sends off roots from its vines where it touches the ground as it's growing, and a piece of vine put in the earth will sprout roots and grow. You can hardly keep this wonderful plant from growing once it gets started. They don't need much nitrogen or other fertilizer, but do appreciate lime in the soil, because they can develop a blackish skin disease called scurf if grown in acid soil.

For many crops, only the biggest and best are saved for seed, but as a hill of sweet potatoes will have all sizes of roots, we can plant the smaller roots that came from healthy plants which were also producing big roots. The compost pile gets the rotten or deformed ones as we sort through the over-wintered baskets in our spring cleaning mode.

You know where the biggest ones go! Washed and slipped into the oven with a big old hickory stick in the fire box, these gems will put smiles on our faces at lunchtime. The rest of the sweet potatoes are laid side by side on the sand and then covered with more sand. I'll put a piece of woven wire over this before I finish covering the whole bed up with sand, three or four inches deep. When we pull the slips, in about six weeks, the wire will hold the potatoes in place, and they will continue to sprout slips for later plantings.

We water the bed well, as the potatoes have been out of the earth since last September and need the moisture to begin their growing. The bed is covered with a row cover, or if it's a cold frame, with window sashes. This makes a small greenhouse which warms up and becomes tropical, just what these South American natives love. Keep the soil moist. In about a month, the little guys will be poking up. Two weeks later, after all danger of frost is past, the slips are pulled from the bed, rinsed off, put in buckets with some water, and taken to the field where they are set about 16 inches apart in rows three and a half feet wide. They are often grown in a ridge.

Bob Woods showed me a sweet potato planting stick. He cut a notch in a stick and attached a #9 wire to it that was eight inches up from the notch and stuck out 16 inches. Lay your slip along the row and push the root down with the notched end of the stick. The end of the wire will show you where to lay the next plant. You can use your feet to firm the soil around the one you just planted. This tool may not sound like much, but it saves the back when planting a few thousand slips. Slips should be planted on a cloudy day just before a rain, since they need water once they are in the ground. They are slow to get going and need to be hoed a few times, but when the summer heat comes, the vines, which have edible leaves, will cover the patch.

A frost will kill the plants, and the vines should be mown down before this, for the potatoes will rot if frosted vines are left on them. We dig them with a potato plow, and after they've dried an hour or two, we put them in boxes and take them to the attic where they cure and are stored. They don't like to be handled a lot, so we move them as little as possible. Sweet potatoes develop their best flavor if they are kept warm, about 85 degrees, for three weeks after they are dug. Then they can be kept in a cool, dry place. Our attic is perfect, because it is warm in the late summer, but cools down when autumn arrives.

Golden Nugget is one of our favorites, a sweet yellow one that has crow-foot leaves, as does the Centennial, another favorite that comes in two colors, red and yellow. Beauregard is a newer, huge producer of large potatoes that are red and moist, but don't keep as well or taste as good. Oklahoma Red has orange flesh and long skinny roots. Both of these kinds have big heart-shaped leaves that are better at shading out the weeds than the narrow-leafed varieties. We've grown a white one called Sumor that is really sweet, and are trying one called Nancy Hall, an old variety I found in Jackson County. All Gold, Puerto Rican, Jewel and Georgia Jet are some of the many others we have grown, and I can say I've enjoyed all of them. But now I grow mostly a local variety Coin Hire's family had been growing for over 100 years. It's the sweetest, best-tasting one we've ever eaten and is also the best keeper.

Whether steamed, baked, boiled or fried, these fall treats are a staple food in our home. When grown on good healthy soil, you won't be adding sugar. They are plenty sweet enough. They've captured the summer sun and turned it into a bright, colorful, delicious food that's enjoyed all over the world, and stores easily until it's time to bed them down again next spring.

October 4, 1994

Hilling

Many vegetables benefit from hilling, or pulling loose soil up around the base of the plant. Come to think of it, the plants that like to be hilled are the American crops. What are the American crops? Corns, beans, squash and potatoes were unknown to Europeans before the discovery of the New World. Of course, many people had already discovered this "new world" and were enjoying these vegetables in their gardens, often hilling them with a dead fish in the hill. The gardens in the Old World must have been boring without four of my favorites. It's interesting that they all like to be hilled.

I've been trying to invent a hiller for my tractor for several years. My first attempt at hilling potatoes was with the potato digger. I offset it so that it followed my right tire. As I straddled the row, it made its trench between the rows, sort of throwing soil up on either side. The first lesson I learned about mechanical hilling is that if you throw the dirt on one side of the row, it pushes the plant over. Back to the drawing board. So, next year, I took apart a gee whiz. I bet more than a few of you have walked behind a gee whiz, which is a one-row, horse-drawn cultivator with many small shovels on it. I put three shovels at an angle on either side of my one-row cultivator (tractor-type), so the shovels closest to the plant were the farthest back. It worked in theory in my head, but not in the field. What I need are small discs, I thought to myself.

Browsing through some potato literature, I ran across an article on hilling potatoes with a potato hiller. I should have figured someone had already been through this. The Maine Potato Growers Association sells handy wing hillers that look like small, adjustable moldboard plows. I put some on an old cultivator and headed for the 'tater patch. We'd just gotten it hoed before the last rain, and the ground was perfect for working. I set the lift down and proceeded to dig up a few yards of potato plants. Oops, too close together. Through trial and error, I finally managed to get them set far enough apart so as to not hurt the plants, but to still throw dirt about halfway up them. I did have to walk up and down a few rows uncovering plants where I'd gotten too close. They looked so pretty when I finished, poking up through their little hills. They looked so good, in fact, that when my cows got out the next day, several rows got their tops eaten off, and cows aren't even supposed to eat potatoes. Don't believe that.

I used the hiller, with a closer spacing, to make the rows for our squash and melon patch. It sure beat making all those little mounds with a rake. We also used it for sweet potato ridges. I'll wait till the corn and beans are ready for their last cultivation and throw some soil up around them, too. The corn, in particular, likes to be hilled so it doesn't blow over in a summer thunderstorm. I usually just pull soil up around the beans as I'm hoeing, preserving moisture while killing weeds. I may have to set the wings farther apart so I don't cover them too much. The higher up you set the wings, the higher the hill is. I've got a lot of fooling around with this new contraption before I learn all the fine points.

The advantages to hilling potatoes and sweet potatoes is that the loose soil is easier for them to make their spuds in. Anytime you raise the earth above ground level, you create a more lively environment because more air is available. More air can also mean more dry, which is why for Irish potatoes, you wait until the plant is half grown. By hilling soil around the plants, you are conserving moisture, and you keep the exposed spuds from turning green. On the other hand, you ridge squash and melons right from the start, because they like to grow in a relatively dry soil. Their deep tap roots get all the moisture they need from the subsoil. Sweet potatoes also like it dry, and their prolific foliage catches plenty of dew. We've made the best sweet potatoes in our driest seasons. Too much rain seems to make them spindly.

I've got extra sweet potato slips to give away. They are in a bucket at the RBS feed store. It's an old-time variety that's been grown in Haysville for almost a century.

June 12, 1998

Flowers

Flowers brighten up the garden, the kitchen, and the face of the one you give them to. They are easy to grow, and you can save the seeds from many of them.

Crocuses are the first harbingers of spring, soon followed by daffodils and other members of the lily family. This family is characterized by flowers with three or six petals, long narrow leaves with veins running lengthwise and propagation by bulbs. Narcissus and grape hyacinth both have a sweet, wild aroma. Irises, with their many showy and different colored blooms, also come in an array of lovely smells; lemony, orange, and my favorite, the root beer flavored ones. A bed of bulbs can have all of these for spring blooms along with gladiola and day lilies for summer color. These plants come back stronger every year from their underground rhizomes and respond well to a mulching of ground bark and compost. They don't like to be planted very deep.

Zinnias come in all colors and sizes. A row in the vegetable garden filled with their rainbow assortment looks stunning. Just plant the seeds when you plant your beans, hoe them once or twice, and soon their blooms will be attracting butterflies and catching eyes. When the flower falls off, a seed head is formed, so one day in September pick a big bag of them, dry them out and store them for next year's garden. They make great cut flowers.

Marigolds also make an easy-to-pick seed head full of distinct white and black, feathery seeds. These are also planted the first week of May, but take longer to start blooming. The odoriferous, dark green foliage helps keep bugs and nematodes out of the garden, so sprinkle a few throughout your vegetables and enjoy their pretty yellows and oranges in late summer.

Cosmos is a fragile looking plant with delicate flowers. The light foliage doesn't cast much shade, so I planted them among the watermelons to add color to that part of the garden. The young plants look like ragweed and can be mistakenly hoed up, as happened to us this year. The rain has brought a heavy peony down, and is also weighing low the giant pink and orange oriental poppies. The smaller, yellow-orange California poppies color up the rose garden, and for true flower lovers, nothing can touch the rose. The white rose and climber didn't die back last winter and are covered in blooms, but it's the hybrid tea roses with their overwhelming aromas that really knock me out.

Many pretty flowers are also good medicines. Echinacea, or purple coneflower, is used as an immune system builder, besides supplying the garden with its gorgeous purple blooms. The root is used to make a tea or tincture. The best medicine is a mixture of two kinds of Echinacea, the common *purpurea* and another one called *augustifolia.* Leave some of the roots in the ground when you dig them, because they will come back every year from the roots, besides reseeding themselves. Chamomile offers delicate yellow and white blooms to make a tea for your tummy. The soothing drink eases a stomachache and is nice to drink at bedtime. Give it a space in your garden, and it will drop its seeds to resprout next season. Most old-time gardens have a spider plant with its purple or pink spidery flowers. It is also known as cleome and is another reseeder. These are the kinds of "weeds" I like; hoe up where I don't want them and leave a few here and there for splashes of color in the landscape.

I couldn't believe how long our hollyhock bloomed this year. It seemed like its spire of pretty pink flowers lasted for months. They also come in shades of red. A stake helps keep this perennial from falling over. For a tall background to the flower bed, you can't beat sunflowers. We used to grow only the Mammoth Russia variety with the edible seeds, most of which were eaten by birds. This year, we have Mexican Red for attracting butterflies, and we've planted many other different sizes and colors of sunflowers. I figure we can save seeds from these if we can beat the birds to them.

Foxglove, cockscomb, four-o'clocks, calendula and the list goes on and on. You can lose yourself in the flower garden, but find new friends. Milkweeds attract monarchs, and honeysuckles get hummingbirds. Vegetables can be grown just for their flowers. Sweet peas and Scarlet runner beans make beautiful blooms, and I like okra flowers better than most okra dishes (except when dipped in cornmeal and fried).

Flowers lighten up your home, adding fragrance and beauty to your life wherever they are. Grow some, pick some, give some; they are always welcomed.

July 13, 1999

Weeds

Weeds have a lot to tell us - usually something we don't want to hear. Why certain plants grow in certain places on the farm can teach us about our soils. Some weeds, like briars, sorrel and broom sedge, thrive on acid soils, and you know you need lime when you see them. A pasture with daisies, fleabane, goldenrod and not much clover could also benefit from some calcium. Pennsylvania smartweed, the weed with knots at every joint that the Japanese beetles love so much, indicates poor drainage and a hardpan. Yellowdock, wild mustard and wild carrots also grow where there is a hard layer of soil below where the plow reaches.

Nature sees that what the land needs, it gets. These deep-rooted plants are there to send a tap root through the hardpan and break it up, allowing access for drainage and air. Then earthworms use the tunnels that are made after the plant dies to transport previously unavailable minerals back up for the plant roots, which eventually find their way deeper. Morning glories, too, speak of a hardpan, and also of crust formation.

When we work the ground when it's too wet, or over-disc or rototill it, a crust often forms on the surface after a hard rain. Thorny-horse nettle likes a crusted soil and won't grow as well where the soil is in good tilth and loose. But if you've just been careless and let your garden go to weeds, it's probably gone to "careless weed," or pigweed. These drought-resistant plants are quite common wherever humans have gardened and they frequent our summer fields.

When Europeans introduced plantain into the Americas, the native people called it the "white man's footsteps," as it grew in the compacted soil where people lived. Sure enough, this low-growing, stringy, leathery-leafed plant is in all our paths and roadways. It does come in handy for its relief of stings, cuts and bruises. Just chew on a leaf and put it on a bee sting and the pain disappears.

Wherever there is decaying organic matter, especially around manure, you'll find lamb's-quarters. The size of this delicious, edible wild spinach will tell you how fertile your ground is. They can get way over your head by summertime, and by then have a white powdery dust on their triangular leaves. The winter-time lover of decaying organic matter is chickweed. These succulent green shoots make a wonderful addition to salads. It covers some beds so thickly in the spring that it needs to be pulled off so the ground will dry out enough to plant.

Land always wants better soil structure, and nature is always willing to send in the grasses to help out. Johnson grass, quack grass, Bermuda grass, goose grass, you-name-it grass are all constant weed problems, especially on crusted soils. But they gradually improve the land with their thatch production. When a properly balanced humus gets formed with the addition of compost and manures, the grasses are weakened and not so much of a problem.

In our lawns, dandelions are sending a deep tap root down to bring up calcium and other minerals to the soil surface. Sometimes it's hard to tell what's a weed and what's not. I may be pulling out clover in a garden spot the same day I'm sowing it somewhere else. I can imagine a science dealing with soil conditions created by specific plant communities, and farmers being able to read their weeds like reading a soil test, just by looking at which weeds are growing where. When I see cocklebur, I know I have plenty of phosphorus, and thistles indicate adequate potassium. My henbit assures me of plenty of organic matter, all of which I appreciate knowing, even though I wish the weeds weren't there.

August 1, 1995

CHAPTER IV

Autumn Arrives

Fall Garden	91
Chinese Cabbage	93
Garlic	96
Putting Foods By	98
Seed Saving	100
Chickpeas	103
Celery	105
Unusual Vegetables	107
Shiitakes	109
Goldenseal and Ginseng	111
Winter Covers	113

> *"Sowing is not so hard as reaping."*
>
> Goethe

Fall Garden

It's time to plant the fall garden. In the height of canning beans, tomatoes and sweet corn, and all the other harvesting, we need to dedicate a few hours to planting. The first frost of autumn is usually in mid-October, but we've seen it as early as September 28 and as late as the first week of November. As of August 4, we have about 70 days until then, maybe more or maybe less. Green beans planted now will make the prettiest beans of all, because the beetles won't be so bothersome late in the season. As the summer wears out, so do the bugs. They just aren't as devouring as they are early on. Weeds aren't nearly as prolific in the fall as they are in the spring and summer either, and the cooler autumn weather makes the fall garden more inviting.

Our broccoli and cauliflower didn't like this summer's extra rainy spells. The compost pile will like them. After pulling them, I got out my trusty garden fork and worked up a couple of rows. Next, I raked it smooth and dug a furrow. Romano bush beans were inoculated and sown four inches apart in rows two feet apart. An old pea patch, taken over by pigweed, ragweed and foxtail, was renovated by bush hogging and using the subsoiler to loosen the weed roots. The fork took care of the rest, and it is now in Blue Lake beans. The chickens get the bolting lettuce stalks, and the old lettuce bed gets new compost. Chinese cabbage goes here for those delicious fall salads, providing heads until the hard winter freezes lay it low. The bok choy goes in the old beet patch, and those old beets were pretty beat.

Grasshoppers are a problem with the newly planted fall garden. It looks like they've eaten our young carrot bed, so we'll have to plant them again. Squash borers have rotted our old crookneck and zucchini squash patch. Planting more in a new location, with a shovel full of old manure under each new hill, insures plenty of squash in September. In another garden we pulled old beans and planted squash, and pulled old squash and planted beans. Rotating crops is a good idea because different plants draw and give different nutrients and forces to the land.

I'd sown Bradley tomato seed between some melon hills in June, and it's time to set them out. A few late tomatoes will produce right up until frost, and provide green ones to put up for ripening later on.

The star of the fall garden is kale. We save our seed by leaving it over winter in the garden and gathering the stalks in June. It is drying up in the barn, and a little stomping and kneading easily yields a quart of small round seeds. As soon as we got three, 300 foot rows of potatoes dug, and with rain threatening, I pulled the rebreaker and harrow through the field. A pass with the subsoiler marked the rows, and then, just as it started to sprinkle, I ran down the rows sprinkling kale seed thinly but steadily. I never did get to rake it in like I planned to, but the rain will see to it.

Again, I'd like to offer our kale seed to anyone who wants to try it. Kale supplies greens from September through the winter, and will come back in the spring with delicious broccoli-like florets. We grow a wide assortment of oriental vegetables. Tendergreen is the common mustard folks grow around here; Mizuna is a lacy-leafed oriental variety. Tatsoi is a small, dark green-leafed, baby Bok choy, and Mei Qing is a pale-green one. Along with a Purple Top turnip patch and a few rutabagas, we grow Japanese daikon radishes such as Misota Rose-flesh, China Rose and Minowase. The fall garden is the prettiest and easiest of all. No bugs, no weeds, and no sweat.

August 4, 1998

Chapter 4 Autumn Arrives

Chinese Cabbage

"The Chinese cabbages that ate Red Boiling Springs" may be the Chronicle headline next week. Neighbors, I'm warning you now, these plants are growing so big that I don't know where they are headed. They are heads and we better eat them up. Actually, it's only the bok choy we need to worry about. We're keeping the other Chinese cabbages under control with big midday salads. We've got to use up all the gleanings from the now defunct tomato and pepper patch, too, which makes early November a great time for eating salads.

In the grocery store, "Napa" is the name given to what I call Chinese cabbages. They are light green with barrel shaped heads weighing four or five pounds apiece. The crinkly, crisp leaves are my favorite salad green, and the stalk is the best part. Oriental folks use them in stir fries, so you've probably had them if you've ever eaten at a Chinese restaurant. We've been growing these hardy annuals since we discovered them in 1975. Gurney's seed catalog offered them as a fall cabbage and we experimented with a few rows. I'll never forget that winter, with not much green anywhere, including the grocery stores, and going out in February to harvest these wonderful, sweet, juicy leaves. A little hay mulch kept them alive through that mild winter, which blew my Northern Illinois (three months of arctic weather) mind. The next winter, `76-`77, was especially hard and cold, and froze our chinese cabbages, and us.

The trick is to get them to sprout and live during the summer drought. The key to the trick is, as usual, compost. A four foot wide garden bed can use a bushel or two of compost for every 10 to 12 feet, annually. The other necessary factor is moisture, but I am not a waterer. Watering is addictive. Once you start, your plants depend on it and wilt if their now too-shallow roots get dry. Instead, I like to keep the sun off of the soil one way or another, to conserve precious soil moisture.

Bean leaves are great for this. Our spring plantings of green beans and shelly beans are well composted, limed, hoed and hilled. Their canopy covers the ground during May and June, with two rows to a four foot bed. After harvesting the beans, I pull the plants by the roots and feed them to the chickens, who love the beetles, or put them in the compost pile. I have other plans for these nice rich bean hills. A quick motion with the rake levels the hills, revealing just enough moisture to sprout a cabbage seed. I have found that cabbages following beans is an appropriate crop rotation. I make a shallow row, and sprinkle the seed by rolling it between my thumb and finger to get three or four per foot. I'll thin them later to a foot apart and either transplant or gobble the thinnings.

Generally speaking, I don't like to walk on the garden beds. It's nice to think of them as fluffy, living beings who need all the air they can get, and who shouldn't be tromped. But rules are made to be broken, and I step right on the freshly covered seeds with my feet, heel to toe, down the row. I want close contact between the seed and the moist soil. Even after a month of no rain, they sprouted and got their first true leaves in a couple of weeks.

The cabbages must have gotten their roots down in there deep, because it was awfully hot and dry, and they stayed alive, although they didn't really grow until it rained a little. Then they jumped up and started doing their thing, which is to make a lovely fall garden. A little bit of weeding is all they need until late October when a hay mulch is tucked around them for protection from hard freezes.

The Chinese cabbages are very cold tolerant and can be kept alive here most winters with a row cover and an old quilt thrown over them if it gets below 10°. Blues is my favorite variety for a nice big head. Lettucy-type is just that, a loose-leaved, lighter green variety looking quite like lettuce. For a big bok choy we grow Joi Choy. Their dark green leaves contrast beautifully with their bright white stalks.

I use a cleaver to finely chop the leaves perpendicular to the veins and then lightly salt them. Olive oil, garlic and parsley dress them in the bowl and, especially with the addition of crumbled feta cheese, you have a wonderful salad. For other flavors, add celery, kale, collards, daikon radishes or any of the many wonderful fall garden vegetables which make such healthy autumn eating.

Chapter 4 Autumn Arrives

But these 10 pound heads of bok choy are weighing heavy on me. Two big leaves sauteed with an onion is plenty for a stir fry, and I just can't eat them everyday like I can the Napas. So if they keep growing, and I don't get some help eating them, I may have to call the RBS Rescue Squad to help protect our town from the invasion of the monster cabbages.

November 9, 1999

Garlic

Garlic is one of our most labor-intensive and profitable crops. We find it a very healthy addition to our diet and use it daily. After a wheat crop last year, we had an undersowing of white Dutch clover until the beginning of August. At that time, I chisel plowed the field and made five beds, each about six feet wide and 100 feet long. I plowed a walkway in between each bed with the moldboard plow. Each bed was given a manure-spreader load of aged compost and a bag of rock phosphate, and then I harrowed in buckwheat seed.

A summertime buckwheat field is an amazing phenomenon to behold. It can sprout without rain and immediately cover the land with lush green seedlings. In three weeks, it can be knee high, and in four to five weeks be in full bloom with a sea of beautiful white flowers. Bees love buckwheat, as do many beneficial insects. It was mown down in mid-September, and the field left for a few days. The soil was rich and soft; buckwheat is famous for its soil improving qualities. A few days later I ran the rebreaker (another name for my 5 shanked chisel plow) through the beds, which made five rows, a foot apart, in each bed.

We sat around the barn for a few days with friends, splitting apart bulbs of garlic into cloves, using only the big bulbs and the unbruised larger-sized cloves, which we then planted five to six inches apart in the rows. The bottom of a garlic clove has to be intact, as that is where the rootlet forms, and we are careful not to plant any cloves with diseased spots on them. After the rows are covered, we fluff up 8 to 10 inches of hay over the whole field, enough to smother weeds, but light enough to let the garlic through. In a month, the garlic is peeking above the mulch and can actually get a foot tall before winter lays it down. It stays green all winter, and first thing in the spring it stands up and starts to grow. At this point, we pull the weeds that have managed to take hold and then remulch the bed. We used nine round bales of hay on this patch altogether.

Our garlic is the Racombole type, which puts out a seed-head in early June. I cut these off with a machete to send a signal to the plant to put its energy into the bulb. We pull the garlic up in late June and immediately clean it, as it is easier to do so before it dries. This involves cutting off the roots and tops with a pruning shears, and peeling the first few sheaths off so that the dirt around the bulb is removed and a nice, clean, red and white garlic bulb is ready for market. We harvest while there are still four or five green leaves on the plant, because each leaf is also a sheath around the bulb, which helps the garlic to store well. By removing only a sheath or two with the dirt on them, we still have a nice cover around the cloves. If you wait until all the leaves are brown, the garlic won't look as pretty.

Our garlic gets 2 1/2 to 3 inches in diameter, but it is not elephant garlic, which is a leek, not a true garlic. We have been saving our own cloves for replanting since the mid-70's, and it is well acclimated to our area. Last year, we tried garlic varieties from eight different countries around the world. Our favorites were Yugoslavian and Spanish Roja. The Italian was quite hot, and the Asian garlic had nice color, but this year we stuck with our own Tennessee stock.

Garlic has anti-bacterial qualities and is recommended by many doctors for people with high cholesterol and other health problems. It seems to keep colds away, it doesn't keep people from wanting to kiss you, and since we've been growing so much garlic here, we've had absolutely no problems with vampires.

July 12, 1994

Putting Food By

Putting food by for winter is one of summer's biggest chores. Root cellars, drying and canning are traditional methods we still use. Many crops will keep through the winter on their own if harvested, cured and stored properly.

Potatoes are dug when the vines die and are quickly laid out in a dark shed, single layer. Any light will turn them green and unfit to eat, so they must always be kept in complete darkness. We check and dispose of rotten ones occasionally until the hard freezes come, and then they are moved in bushel baskets to the root cellar. Onions and garlic are pulled, laid out to dry, then hung in an airy spot till late fall, when they are moved inside the house or chicken coop. A cool dry place that won't freeze hard is ideal for them. Winter squash and pumpkins are kept in the barn till it starts freezing, then moved into the house in baskets. Turnips and beets are taken to the root cellar in late fall with the tops removed and the roots left on. Apples are also taken to the cellar, and they need to be checked routinely for bad ones. Jerusalem artichokes keep well there, too.

We use a solar dryer to dry mushrooms, apples, pears, tomatoes, yellow squash, sweet corn, broccoli, peppers and the garlic we want to grind into garlic powder. It is simply an insulated two-foot square box with a hinged window on top and a screen shelf inside. The vegetables are tough, but soften when cooked and they're great added to soups and stews. We slice the produce thinly and lay it on a screen. It is usually done in a few days. We tried drying carrots and beets, but they turned out too rubbery. Apples are often dried outdoors on a roof or in an old car with the windows up. A sheet of cheesecloth over them keeps the flies off. They are done when they feel dry and crack when bent. Herbs are usually cut in the morning after the dew dries and before the plant is in full bloom, then hung upside down in a dark attic or placed loosely in paper sacks and hung in the kitchen. When they have thoroughly dried, we strip the leaves off the stems and store them in jars.

For canning, the jars are washed and scalded, and the lids washed and put into a pan of hot water. Loosely pack the jars (pints, unless

Chapter 4 Autumn Arrives

otherwise noted) with fresh, clean vegetables and fill with boiling water. Put the lids on and pressure cook at ten pounds pressure:

- Peas for 40 minutes
- Corn for 55 minutes
- Green beans for 25 minutes (quarts)
- Pinto beans for 40 minutes

Salt can be added to each jar, but is not necessary for preserving the food. We started canning our shell beans, too, after we lost a gallon jar of dried black-eyed peas to worms. We fill a pint jar halfway with field peas, soybeans, October beans or whatever we have, and then fill the jar with boiling water and pressure cook them for 40 minutes.

Tomatoes are scalded, peeled and packed into quart jars like other vegetables, then put into a big kettle of boiling water for 45 minutes. This is called a "water bath". They don't have to be pressure canned. Tomatoes also can be made into a sauce by cooking them down with onions, peppers, garlic, oregano, basil and any other seasonings you want, then processing them for 15 minutes.

Fruits are put into quart jars and filled with almost-boiling honey-water, made by warming eight parts water to one part honey. Put the jars in a water bath for 15 minutes. We do cherries, blackberries, grapes, blueberries, raspberries and pears this way, and it makes great fruit juice. Apples can be turned into applesauce and water bathed for 20 minutes or pressed into cider and canned in half-gallon jars in a water bath for 30 minutes.

Jellies, jams, preserves, pickled beets, soups and even meats can also be put up in jars when produce is plentiful. All vegetables should be fresh, ripe, clean, and put into the jars immediately. Leave 1/4 to 1/2-inch of room at the top of the jar when you fill them with liquid, and be sure to wipe the rim before putting the top on. Hand tighten the band. Process the jars right away, and when you take the jars out, let them set for a day to cool and dry off. Then label and store in a cellar or dark pantry. We take the rings off so they don't rust and stick. It's a joy, when the winter winds blow, to be able to open up a jar of summer.

August 3, 1994

Seed Saving

Seed saving is an important, economical and educational part of gardening. Sometimes it's the only way you can have a certain vegetable variety, because seed catalogs are rapidly dropping many of the old varieties. The genetic makeup of various varieties of seed is different, and when a variety becomes extinct, those particular genes are gone for good. Plant breeders use and need a wide variety of plants in their work, so it is important to keep as many different kinds of plants around as possible.

Because plants are rooted to the ground and can't leave when conditions are unfavorable, they compensate by giving their offspring more strength to deal with a particular environment. This has caused the great diversity in plant species since different climates create a different variety of the same genus. Up North, only the cold-hardy plants survive to make seed, whereas in the South, a plant must be able to withstand long, hot summers and drought.

We save butternut squash seed every year, and now it is well adapted to our farm. It is no longer bothered by squash bugs and borers and reliably makes a good crop. We take the seeds out before we cook the squash and dry them in a pie plate on a windowsill. There are four species of squash and pumpkins, all in the *Cucurbitas* family. Crossing occurs easily within the same species, but rarely with other species.

C. pepo are all the summer squash, plus acorn, spaghetti, delicatas and Connecticut field pumpkins. Don't save your seed like I did two years ago and end up with a field of pumpkin-acorn crosses that were either dark green pumpkins or inedible, huge, odd-shaped monster squash. *C. maxima* are the large pumpkins and buttercup squash. They are sensitive to a wilt disease. *C. mixta* are the green-striped cushaw grown in the South years ago. They are quite drought-tolerant and are grown in Mexico where the seeds are roasted and eaten. *C. moschata* are the butternuts, Tennessee pumpkins and Tahitian melon. If the species (the last word of the Latin name) is the same for two plants, the squashes will cross-pollinate and not come back as a true variety.

I am saving Charleston Grey watermelon seeds from a patch that was far from my other watermelons, but I'm not saving any of the others, because they were all grown together and would not necessarily come true. Beans are easy to save, and there are many old varieties handed down from generation to generation. It's sad for me to hear of old varieties that have been locally grown for years and are adapted to our climate, then are lost when an old-timer passes away. To save bean seeds, just let the beans dry on the plant and thresh out what you need. Beans don't readily cross, so if your varieties have a little distance between them, you are okay. Tomatoes also come true easily, but only save seed from non-hybrids. Hybrid seeds revert back to a parent without the hybrid's characteristics, so we don't save hybrid seed.

Tomato and cucumber seeds need to undergo a fermentation process, so I just squish up some of the fruits in a bucket of water, then screen out the seeds after a few days. They are rinsed, dried, packed into jars and labeled. Kale seed is also easy to save, but needs to be separated from other brassicas, as it will cross with them. The over-wintered plants will send up a seed stalk, and when the pods are ripe, we cut, dry and thresh them. One plant can make many seeds. Garlic is propagated by cloves, not seeds, and we save only the biggest bulbs for planting. This way, we have gradually improved our stock by only using the healthiest and largest bulbs for replanting.

Open-pollinated corn is easy to save, also. We have some Indian corn that is quite drought tolerant and makes very good corn meal. The old varieties often have better flavor, disease resistance and other characteristics that benefit home gardeners, whereas the commercial varieties are bred for ease of mechanical harvest or transportation. Only recently have gardeners begun to rely on purchased seed. This seed often is grown in specific conditions with chemical fertilizers and pesticides added. It may fail in a more natural environment under different conditions where a locally adapted variety would thrive.

A great percentage of the old varieties have been lost already, and the race is on to save the ones that are left. So, if you have a seed that's been in the family awhile, find a seed bank, or a young gardener, and ensure that it continues on. You learn a lot about a plant when you complete the cycle by saving its seeds from year to year. Besides saving a little money, you contribute to the important work of maintaining our vanishing vegetable heritage.

September 15, 1994

Chickpeas

Chickpeas are a common food in the Middle East, where they are often ground into flour and made into a paste called "hummus." As we love to experiment with varieties of unusual plants, I shouldn't have been surprised when a box of them showed up in the mail. But I was. Ten varieties of chickpeas from Afghanistan, India, Bulgaria, Yugoslavia and Iran had mysteriously been sent to me. The next day, a letter from my friend Donna explained it. Our local organic gardening club had the seeds to do a research project, so she sent some of them to try in our garden.

I've seen chickpeas, also called garbanzo beans, in the health food stores where we market our vegetables. They are large, light-tan beans that look like big peas. Opening the packets revealed two varieties I could recognize as garbanzos; the others were small and brown and looked more like a wrinkled vetch seed. After the plants had sprouted, we immediately noticed they looked like vetch and, upon looking it up in our horticultural encyclopedia, we found they indeed were closely related to the common hairy vetch we grow as a winter cover crop.

On May 11 the field was already composted, and we were planting October beans, pinto beans and some of the old-time bean varieties our neighbors had given to us. I had no idea how to plant a chickpea, so I just sowed them rather thickly in a row next to the other beans, with sticks in between to mark the different varieties. A couple of passes with the cultivator and hoe were quite sufficient to produce an abundant crop of chickpeas. But several of the small pods, which only had two small peas (or are they beans?) in them also had insect holes. Even though chickpeas were from the other side of the world, some local insects found a liking for them. This, coupled with the desire to plant the fall kale in this spot, led me to harvest the hairy, bushy plants and label them in boxes to further dry in the barn. A damp spell in summer means moldy beans, and the dry-climate chickpeas suffered. I may have harvested them too early (mid-July), but they might have molded in the field anyway. We shelled them by hand, and I'm convinced that Middle Eastern farmers either have much more patience and time than I do, or else they use a combine.

These beans (or are they peas?) are tiny, with only two in each pod. An Iranian variety yielded the best-looking beans, the big tan garbanzo bean like I'd seen in stores. The other one from Iran was prolific, but the seeds were very small and black. The biggest plants, Ploudou 19 from Bulgaria, proved to be the most worthless, with only a very few, tiny seeds. Maybe it's used as a cover crop or for livestock grazing. The other Bulgarian one, Obrazcou Ciflik, produced large black beans, lots of them, and was probably the second best for usable food. The Afghanistan, Indian and Pakistan varieties had small brown seed of not much use. Yugoslavia Krnjveski (I'd like to hear you pronounce that) was also small. Another Yugoslavian variety, Lokalen, had the nice big tan beans, but had gotten moldy.

All in all, I'd say they are a dry-weather crop, and would produce well here in a dry year. They are probably best harvested and thrashed more like a grain crop rather than hand-shelled. For us, they could make a good summer cover crop or be used for cattle feed. One of the nice things about our research project was to hear the names of these countries in connection with something besides a war or natural disaster. While tending these plants I imagined farmers in Pakistan, Yugoslavia or Iran hoeing their crops just as we do. Maybe everybody over there isn't involved in shooting each other.

I pressure-cooked the seeds for 40 minutes and tasted the different varieties. The large tan ones were the best - soft, tender and flavorful, almost like boiled peanuts. The large black ones were tougher (they may need longer cooking time) with a stronger flavor. The small brown and black ones were also not as tender. Maybe these are the kind that are ground to make hummus. These seeds have been passed down from year to year in Middle Eastern families, just like we do with our bean seeds. Although I may never grow these varieties again, it was a fun and tasty experiment.

September 2, 1996

Celery

Celery is a common enough vegetable, but often ignored by home gardeners. We love it and have grown it for many years, enjoying the crisp stalks in salads and soups. The seed is very small and, like other members of the umbrella family, slow to germinate.

In March, we sprinkle the seed in a flowerpot with a mixture of sand, compost and soil, then pat the seeds down and lightly sprinkle with water. Tender shoots finally appear after a few weeks and, when the first true leaves come out, we transplant them to individual soil blocks or cups. After all danger of frost is past, they are set out in the richest soil we can find. Commercial celery is grown in mucky soils with high fertility and lots of organic matter, so we give our celery plenty of compost. We dig a hole and fill it with compost before transplanting, and then keep the ground loose and friable around the plants. In a dry year we mulch them because celery does not like dry weather at all.

This family attracts beneficial insects, so we always have some in the garden. I've never seen a bug on celery growing outside and have not had many disease problems either, except that towards the end of the year the inside of some of the plants starts to rot and turn black. I don't know if it's a disease or the natural dying of the plant at the season's end. In September we transplant a few plants into the greenhouse, where they supply us with stalks all winter long. Aphids and white flies will get on them here inside, and by spring the plants are pretty well eaten by us and them. Some people blanch them so they turn white, by covering the stalks with soil or wrapping them with paper or something to keep the light out. With no light, the plants don't make chlorophyll, which is what makes them green. We have no problems with green celery. It's less work and actually more flavorful.

Ventura is our favorite variety. We've tried the old-time Golden Self-Blanching and Utah, but they didn't do as well. Like most vegetables, the flavor of homegrown celery is miles above celery from the supermarket. The crunchy stalks are really at their best in the fall after a few cool spells. We still have some outdoors in mid-November that we throw an old sheet over on the nights when it freezes hard.

An interesting relative of celery is celeriac, which is grown for its edible root. The crown just underground swells up like a turnip, and has the same unmistakable celery flavor. The leaves of celery can be used to flavor soups and dried for use as an herb. There's a variety called cutting celery grown just for the leaves. Celery seed is also used as a flavoring in some dishes, but we've never over-wintered it so that this biennial could make its seed. Pile up some manure and weed stalks in a corner of a garden bed this fall and in the spring work it into the ground. We'll give you a few celery plants and you can try your luck with this wonderful, delicious and slightly obscure vegetable.

November 26, 1996

Unusual Vegetables

Ready for a change? Tired of the same old thing? There are many unusual vegetables around that can add excitement to your garden. Kohlrabi looks like a broccoli plant, but instead of the flower bud swelling, it is the stem that swells up. The stalk can get as fat as a turnip, and it sort of tastes like one, too. We eat it raw with salt, and it can be cooked up in a stew. All kinds of oriental brassicas decorate our fall garden, from dark green tatsoi to the light green and feather-leafed mizuna. Chinese cabbage, bok choy, daikon radish, kale, collards, rutabagas and turnips are all in the same family.

Lettuce and spinach taste so good right now, but will bolt as soon as summer comes. Swiss chard, a relative of beet that's called a "silver beet" in Europe, is a luscious green that grows all summer long. It comes in ruby red, orange and yellow colors, too. We've grown New Zealand spinach, which is not a relative of real spinach. It makes a carpet of triangular leaves that are thick and edible during hot weather. Another tropical green is Basella, a vine we tried for the first time last year. It grew up a cane tipi and made slick, dark green leaves for salads and greens. The hot weather just makes it grow better, and it has reseeded itself, so I'll just let it have a little place in our garden.

Asparagus bean, or yard-long bean, seems to be a relative of black-eye peas. It has the same lush, leathery foliage, and the pods are similar, although much longer. But even though they are a couple of feet long, they can be chopped up to make good string beans. Additionally, they are more resistant to drought and insects. The frost hardy Fava beans are planted early in March, while Christmas limas, soy butterbeans and black-eye peas love the heat and are planted in June.

It guess it's a fact of life that most kids love spaghetti and hate squash. Try some spaghetti squash this year. After you bake the large, yellow oval fruits, remove the seeds and spoon or fork out the strings of flesh. It looks just like spaghetti and is rather bland flavored, so that with some spaghetti sauce on it you have a new twist on a spaghetti dinner. Gourds offer an amazing selection of fun things to grow. From dippers to bird-houses, miniature pumpkins to bushel baskets, ugly warty monsters to colorful ornamental decorations, you can let your vines crawl all over the garden or up a trellis. You can grow a luffa and make your own sponges.

Peanuts are another fun crop. The pea-like plants make little yellow flowers that send a shoot down into the earth where the peanut is formed. We like the Virginia peanut better than the Tennessee variety, regardless of the name. The plants are dug in the fall, flipped over and left to dry in the field. They are delicious either boiled in salt water or roasted in the oven.

Fennel is a celery-sized plant that you also eat the stalk of, but with a very different flavor. It tastes like licorice or anise, and the feathery leaves are quite attractive. Parsnips are an old English vegetable that's not grown much around here. The sweet white roots need a winter to ripen, so although they are planted now in springtime, we don't eat them until next February and March, when something from the garden is especially welcome.

In the onion family, leeks are a delicacy, but they are another slow grower. To get the long white stalks, you plant them in rich black soil and hill them up as they grow. Chives and garlic chives are easily grown, and there are many kinds of green bunching onions and shallots, all growing best in the cooler months. Eggplants and tomatillas belong to the same heat-loving family as the wide variety of luscious tomatoes and flavorful peppers.

To color up your meals, try blue potatoes, golden beets, purple string beans, burgundy okra, rainbow sweet corn, white cucumbers and yellow watermelons. Lettuce also comes in colors from green to reds, and even a spotted variety called Freckles. Their shapes range from round Icebergs to barrel-shaped Romaines, Oak leaf to Bibbs and many kinds of loose-leafed varieties.

For nostalgia and history, try some of the old Indian and heirloom varieties of beans, corn, tomatoes and squash. Every seed has an old story to tell, and we can experience something new in our gardens every year.

May 9, 1996

Shiitakes

Shiitakes are gourmet mushrooms anyone can grow easily at home. They were illegal in this country until recently because of a name confusion with a different mushroom that ate railroad ties. With that cleared up, it's time they became more widespread, as they are in Japan where they are a staple food. It's heartening to think of using our forests to produce such a highly nutritious food. Shiitakes supply us with protein, vitamins and minerals from oak logs, which would otherwise be unavailable. Add to this the health benefits of a strengthened immune system against degenerative diseases and you have a very valuable crop. Best of all, they're delicious!

We start by thinning out small white oak trees during October when the sap starts falling. Woodlots often contain crooked trees or ones growing too close together. I never cut a tree that has a chance to make a big, beautiful specimen. To answer a common question, you can't use already dead wood. The tree must be inoculated with Shiitake spawn soon after it's cut, because other mushroom spawn will be trying to get in there and you don't want contamination.

I cut the logs into three or four foot lengths; three foot if it's diameter is seven or eight inches and longer for the thinner ones. You want your logs to be light enough for easy handling. Any hardwood will grow Shiitakes, but white oak is the most recommended and consequently the only one I've used. We've used up over 400 logs in the last 10 years and hope to plug another 100 this fall.

The next step is to tuck in my long beard and drill 7/16-inch holes an inch deep into the logs. I drill the holes six inches apart, lengthwise down the log, in rows 1-1/2 inches from each other in a diamond pattern. Each hole is filled with mushroom spawn, which is the mycellium growing in a sawdust medium. Mushrooms are non-flowering plants which reproduce from spores dropped from the mushroom gills. These spores are grown in a clean laboratory and then used to inoculate sawdust, which then gets a white mold on it. This is the mycellium, which we could compare to mushroom roots. We want the whole log to be filled with it.

The spawn is also available in plug form, a little easier to use and a little more expensive. But for the amount of mushrooms you get it is all relatively cheap; $20 does about 30 logs and will give you Shiitakes for many years. I sell them for $7 a pound. The catch is you have to wait about a year before you get your first one.

Food grade cheese wax or paraffin is softened on the stove and smeared over the filled holes to seal them up. Now the logs are stacked in the deep woods, and left for a year. Check them the next September, and if you see a white ring around the ends of the logs, you know the mycellium has grown through it and they are ready to fruit.

We have to shock them into fruiting, and this is done by soaking the logs in water overnight. We use the creek or a pond, but a bathtub would work if you let your water set for a day to let the chlorine dissipate. After 24 hours in the water, the logs are leaned up against a tree or a board in the woods with about 70% shade. Within two weeks, they are covered with beautiful mushrooms. After harvest, the logs are left to rest for a few months, then soaked and fruited again. They will make mushrooms for several years, although less and less as the spawn eats the logs and they get lighter.

When harvested, the stems are taken off and the mushrooms cut into strips, dipped in egg, and rolled in cornmeal that may have a little cayenne and oregano added to it. After a few minutes in hot oil on the stove, they are salted and devoured with gusto. They are also great in stir fries, soups and on pizzas, or anyway you would use other mushrooms.

Imagine our woods being too valuable to cut for timber because of all the food we are growing in them. Along with Shiitakes, the world's best ginseng and goldenseal can be grown, making our forests capable of producing annual incomes much greater than what we get from logging, which only pays once in a generation. I've enjoyed working with these crops in the shade much more than my field crops during this hot, late summer day.

September 14, 1999

Goldenseal and Ginseng

Goldenseal and Ginseng are a couple of small perennial herbs, native to our woods, that have great value as healing plants. Many people dig and sell the roots; so much so, that they are getting hard to find. But I ran across a big goldenseal patch yesterday and dug a handful for our medicine chest. We use it for healing cuts and wounds, sinus problems, and as a cure for the common cold.

Yellowroot, another name for goldenseal, grows in the rich humus of a deep, shady woods. The foot tall plant has two, five-lobed, serrated leaves about the size of a small hand. The smaller one is on a leaf stalk, and the upper one is attached to the stem. You know you've found yellowroot when you dig just below the plant and pull up a bright yellow root. It's a small, knotty rhizome not more than an inch and a half long, about a half-inch thick, with a strong, bitter odor that's unmistakable. This grove of big oak, maple and beech trees, with their arching branches and the light filtering through the leaves, was like a great cathedral with a sacred feeling in it.

One rule of herb gathering is always leave more than you take, so I just dug a few of the bigger plants for our medicine, and also got a few smaller ones to transplant elsewhere. I took the roots down to the creek and spent a good while scraping and cleaning them, removing all the soil. Now they are in a basket above the wood cook stove, drying. We'll grind them in a grain mill and use the powder on open cuts and scrapes. Goldenseal is an antiseptic, and I sometimes mix it with honey for a healing salve.

The last time I harvested goldenseal, I broke the root in half and the part with the leaf still attached was planted in a different place, and they all lived. I cleaned the other roots well, and ground them in a hand-operated grain mill until I got about one cup of goldenseal powder. I put it in a quart jar and filled the jar with a mixture of 70% pure moonshine and 30% water. I shook the jar every day for about a month or so, and then poured off the liquid and filled 2 ounce dropper bottles with it. We use it as an antiseptic for cuts, on toothaches, or to fight the flu. If the goldenseal don't cure you, the moonshine will!

It is unsurpassed for helping with the common cold. A teaspoon of goldenseal powder in a cup of boiling water is a relief for a cough and snotty nose, although, like most medicines, it tastes terrible (and benefits from some honey). Debby actually sniffs the powder up her nose for sinus problems. I used it with boric acid for an eyewash when I had a sty, and it's used as an ear drop for earaches. Herbalists have told us if they could only have one herb on hand, it would be goldenseal.

In and amongst the goldenseal patch, I spotted the bright red berries of a small ginseng plant. I replanted the seeds, but left the two-pronger to grow, as I only dig three or four-pronged ginseng. The five, finely toothed leaflets, about a foot off the ground, are on two, three or four prongs, depending on how old the plant is. You can count the rings on the distinctively flavored root to see how many years it's been growing. 'Sang is worth a lot now, and as a cash crop it looks to be very promising. Wild ginseng from Appalachia is the most valuable in the world; it goes to China where its medicinal qualities are revered.

A root that looks like a man is particularly coveted in China, where ginseng is used to increase vitality, relieve mental and physical fatigue, dissolve tumors and prolong life. We just chew on the roots or make a vibrant tea out of them, but don't really use it to cure anything specific. You can buy ginseng seeds and try to get a patch going.

The seeds are stratified in a sandbox with an open bottom to let rain through. They need a year and a half before they'll sprout. They grow in a rich soil on a slope, often facing north. The seeds are spaced about a foot apart, and the other plants cleared out from around them. The seedlings are a small, three-leafed plant that is easily trampled by wildlife. It takes at least four years to get a good sized plant; it's more like seven to ten years before they're ready to dig, and it takes even longer for the most valuable ones. Many other useful herbs grow wild in our forest and fields and can be encouraged to expand their patches, and give us good reason to protect these natural resources.

September 17, 1996

Winter Covers

The gardens are tucked in their beds, with the autumn breezes whistling sweet bedtime tunes. We can really promote health and vigor in next year's gardens by giving them a warm blanket for the winter's night. I'm trying several different "quilts" this fall, in an attempt to determine fall cover crop strategies. Experimenting is what keeps me going. There is so much to learn from nature, and I feel like she appreciates an inquisitive mind. But the various weather extremes make one year all too short for conclusions. A cold winter may kill a cover crop which would have thrived in a mild one.

Rye and vetch have always been my main winter cover crop combination. Annual rye is a grain, similar to wheat, with a little more rank growth. It's famous for its root system. This massive fibrous root holds the soil, creates great soil structure and sucks up nutrients that might otherwise leach away. Purple hairy vetch has a great name, doesn't it? It's a legume and a climber, so when it's sown with the rye, it climbs up the sturdy rye stalks. At the same time, its deep top root glides right past the rye's extensive, upper-layer root system, and burrows down into the deeper soil layers where it breaks up the hardpan. As an added bonus, vetch fixes atmospheric nitrogen into the garden through a symbiotic relationship with soil bacteria.

I pour the rye into a five-gallon bucket, about half-full, and toss in two cupped handfuls of vetch, mixing them together. Then, I pour more rye in and another double handful of vetch and mix it all together. I used to use 10# of vetch for every 50# bushel of rye, but when vetch seed prices rose, I found 5# per bushel of rye sufficient. The rye is the bulk and vetch the sweetener. One vetch plant can climb up the rye and spread over several square yards, so you really don't need more than 10% vetch in your mix. Sowing seed by hand is one of my favorite farming chores. The fall colors are peaking as I rhythmically walk and toss the seed in a high arc, opening my hand and letting it scatter in a 10 or 12 foot wide swath. I try to make each throw like the last one and cover about half an acre with each bushel.

Last year's corn patch got spaded, as did a small hayfield beyond it. The next three fields did not get the spader, but had the rebreaker run through them three times. I'm trying to ascertain how much fall tillage we need to get a good stand of the cover crop. A friend gave me two bushels of crimson clover seed he had harvested, so all my buckets got a few handfuls of that mixed in. The bright red flowers in May are strikingly beautiful, and this clover is also a nitrogen-fixing legume. Some of the fields received only crimson clover to give us a pure stand of pretty flowers next spring. It's a great crop to plow in for a late corn patch. One field has wheat mixed in with the crimson clover. It was planted late, so I hoped the wheat would help nurse the clover through the winter. I'm not too worried about the earlier plantings, as they already have made substantial fall growth.

Crimson clover now has eased into the number-one slot on my all-star hit parade of winter cover crops. As a calcium-loving plant, it thrived on the lime spread in the fall, and also enjoyed the moist spring weather. A native of southern Europe, crimson clover is quite adapted to our climate. It is highly esteemed as a cover crop in orchards. Red clover is a different plant, having a more purplish bloom (which is used as an herbal medicine in teas and tinctures) and is grown in longer rotations for a hay crop, and White Dutch clover is sown in our pastures.

One field has oats as the nurse crop for the clover, but this wasn't what I'd planned. A co-op mistakenly gave me a bushel of oats when I thought I'd bought a bushel of wheat. Oh well, another chance to experiment. Oats are more easily winter killed, which could be an advantage if the clovers get well established, but a disadvantage if they don't.

Red clover is sown where I don't want to till next year, but instead want to grow a hay crop. Fescue will sneak in on its own, so I just mixed a couple of pounds of red clover with a bushel of rye and tossed it out on the rebroken, old corn field. All of the fields get the spike-tooth harrow, or at least an old log drag, run over them to cover the seed.

Another great soil-building cover crop is also good-eating: turnips. They make a lot of leaf, and their roots loosens the ground. A relative, Daikon radish, is even better because of its deeper root and is a good addition to the cover crop mix. Rape, the plant canola oil is made from, is another member of this mustard family used as a cover crop. Last year we used Austrian peas instead of vetch because that's what the feed store had the day we were planting. It worked just as well, climbing up the rye and making pretty pea plants. I let some go to seed in the butternut patch and may get a stand of them there again. Vetch is also notorious for reseeding, but it is hoed out easily enough, and if it's not in the way, it is making the ground more fertile, so more power to it.

Leaving the ground bare all winter is like forgetting to tuck your children in bed at night. A few dollars' worth of seeds will save soil, build humus, give your gardens and fields a nice green blanket, and give you a nice warm feeling.

October 26, 1998

Stinging Nettle

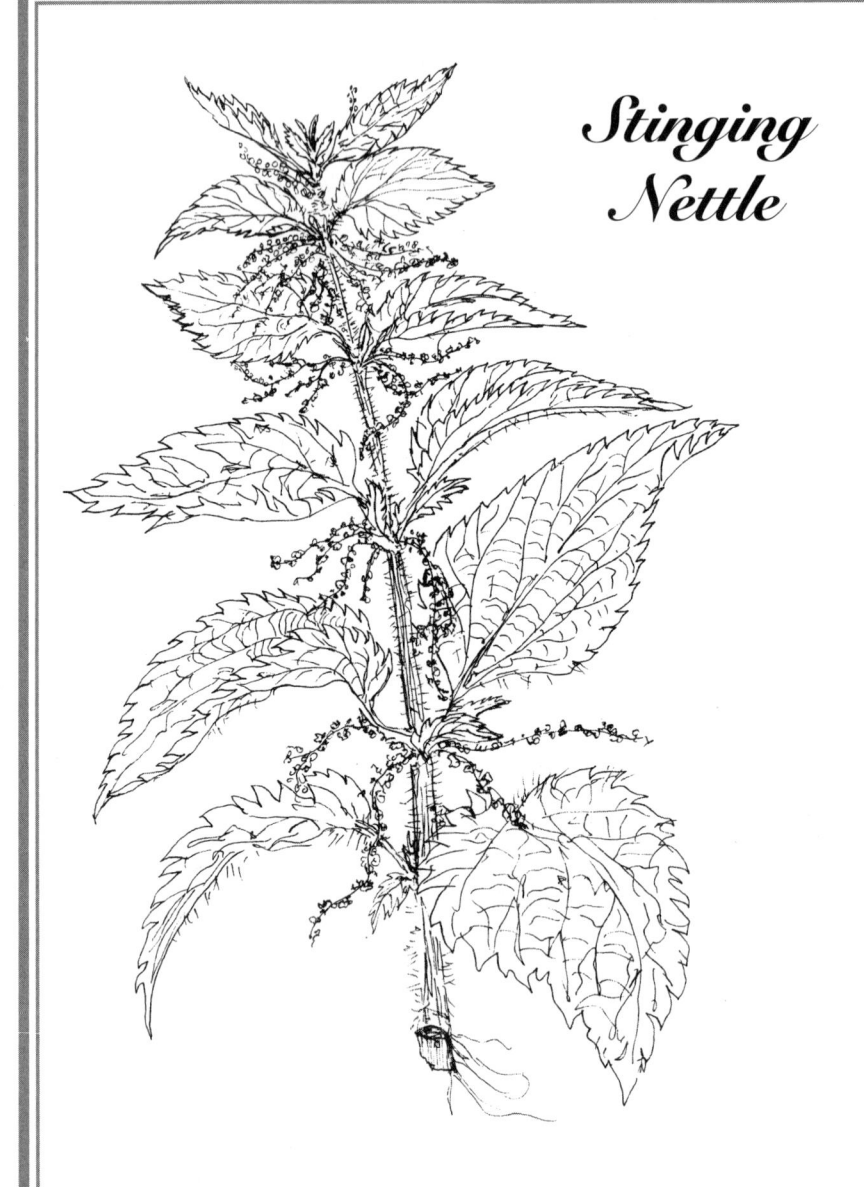

Urticaceae Urtica dioica

CHAPTER V

Berries and Fruit

Raspberries	119
Blueberries	121
Strawberries	123
Mulberries	125
Pears	127
Apples	129
Pruning	131
Grafting	133
Top Working	135
Persimmons	137
Wine	139
Cider	142

> *"These trees shall be my books."*
>
> Shakespeare

Raspberries

Red raspberries are the fruits of the gods. Their heavenly taste and unique aroma are almost too divine for us mere mortals. My first raspberry experiences were in the patch our family had along the woods in Illinois. Mom would send us kids out to pick the berries, knowing full well we'd eat most of them and she'd be lucky to get enough for a pie. Actually, she was probably just trying to get us out of her hair. Those same plants made it down here to our famous red raspberry patch up on the hill. We'd lose apples to late frosts, mulberries to the birds and grapes to the deer, but we could always count on a good raspberry crop.

There are four colors of raspberries - red, black, yellow and purple, which is a cross between the red and the black. The wild blackcaps with their light purple canes grow in the woods around here. The red raspberries grow wild in more northern states. A virus that the wild blackcaps carry will not affect them, but will kill the red ones. Our red patch was wonderful until I let some black ones grow up nearby and then the red ones went into a decline and never recovered. I had to learn the hard way to keep the two separated.

We set the young sprouts, dug from the old patch, about two feet apart in the row in a well-drained, composted garden bed. We used rotten sawdust and old hay for mulch. Most raspberries are biennial, which means the canes sprout up one year and bear fruit and die the next. Pruning consists of taking out the old dead canes and topping the one-year shoots at about four feet. We had a wire trellis on either side of the row to keep them from falling over.

Fall Gold is the yellow variety we tried and loved, until they died back one harsh winter. We've grown Latham, Newburgh, Mammoth and several other red varieties, but have settled on our favorite - Heritage. What makes Heritage so good, besides its great flavor, is its ease of maintenance. The canes are mown down in the fall, composted and mulched, and then come back next year to make a huge fall crop. Unlike most red varieties that bear in June on two-year canes, these bear no spring crop and require no special pruning. It was the Japanese beetles that put the final end to our original berry patch, eating berries and leaves when they came out. The beetles are about gone by the time the Heritage starts producing in August and September, so they don't do much damage to them.

We collect raked and bagged leaves every fall (you can leave your leaf bags at the dump or let me know and I'll come get them) to mulch our patch. They sprout right up through it in the spring and don't need much other care. Red raspberries send out suckers, and these we dig up and sell to our nursery customers. I've propagated them from root cuttings, also, which are made by cutting 4 inch sections of the roots and lining them out in the garden in early spring. Black and purple raspberries are propagated by tip layering, which means that the tips of the canes make new plants by rooting where they lean over and touch the ground. Our purple ones are huge, growing 12 or 15 feet before they arch back down to the earth.

Mom made lots of jams and jellies, but none better than her raspberry. Dad was still tending his patch and bringing her raspberries when in his eighties. Raspberry pies and raspberry wine are two of the many ways we enjoy these heavenly fruits.

Bushhogging the orchard yesterday found me hot and dry on a beautiful October afternoon. The raspberry patch was full, and soon so was I. A flood of raspberry experiences flashed before me, and I hope to always have a berry patch nearby.

October 15, 1996

Blueberries

Blueberries make me say, "Where am I?" Usually, I think I'm in the South, but when it comes to blueberries, it can be confusing. My experience now indicates that the northern varieties do better here than the southern ones. I didn't have this confusion in 1983 when we set out 100 southern "rabbit-eye" blueberries. Over the years, I've replaced lost ones with the northern "highbush" varieties, Bluecrop and Collins, and now feel like they are more suited to our place. It was while admiring a Mennonite farmer's huge blueberry bushes that I realized my mistake. His were the northern ones, and they looked better than my southern ones. Tifblue, Climax, Garden Blue and Southland were the rabbiteye varieties that we set out. They thrive at Hector Black's farm 35 miles to the south, but here I'm going with some more of the northern varieties, including Blueray and Bluejay. I also set out four Ozark Blues, a new cross between the northern and southern varieties.

On a bluff overlooking the Long Fork Creek, I once found wild huckleberries, along with mountain laurel, a member of the rhododendron family. These are the acid-soil lovers, and point to the major soil condition in growing blueberries - a low pH. Blueberries' shallow root system needs to be in soil with a pH of about five, so an ounce of sulfur is used in each hole if the land has a pH of 6.5. I used peat moss mixed with compost to fill in the holes for our patch. The ground had been manured and plowed in the fall with some leaves and old sawdust mixed in, so all we had to do was loosen the soil and remove the grass clumps.

The plants were set into the mixture with an equal amount of soil. We firmed the bushes in with a footstep and then watered them. Now there are three more blueberry beds, 12 feet apart with five feet between the plants in the row. I'll mulch the beds with black sawdust and mow between the rows with the bushhog. Blueberries don't need much pruning at first. Just let them grow into a bush, and (the hardest part of all) pick off the blooms for a year or two to let the plant put its energy into vegetative growth. After they start bearing, you can remove a few inside branches to let light into the center. Of course, all diseased and dead wood is removed, along with lower branches that are too shaded.

Mulch is a must for keeping the soil moist, and the acid mulches are the best. Well-rotted sawdust, wood chips or bark work great. Spread it around each plant four to six inches deep and out to the drip line. Blueberries suffer from high soil temperatures and drought, both of which a mulch will help to alleviate, and they absolutely love organic matter. Don't use lime which would raise the pH. Cottonseed meal is an acid fertilizer blueberries love, but I don't love it because of the way cotton is raised. As a non-food plant, cotton receives more pesticides than I can begin to imagine, and these concentrate into the cotton seed. So cottonseed meal is not for me. I'd consider soybean meal, though I'm cautious of the genetic engineering soybeans can receive, so I'll just stick with good old compost. Besides, it's free.

Once your plants are established, fruit buds form in the fall, and if they aren't winter killed, will flower the following spring. All the honeybees in the world won't help you now, for blueberries need bumblebees for pollination. Some butterflies help, too, as it takes a long proboscis to get into the deep blueberry blossom. Blueberries like a well-drained soil with plenty of sun, although a bit of afternoon shade is all right. As they bear in July, irrigation is important for a commercial planting to make bigger berries. We count on a good mulch and healthy plants to make it through dry spells.

With blueberry muffins, pancakes, pies, jams, juice and fresh in yogurt or on cereal, you won't need help figuring out how to enjoy them. I'm a northerner transplanted in the South, kind of like my blueberries. Sometimes when I have a tummy full of blueberries, I forget everything and wonder, "Where am I?" but, like any satisfied animal, I'm just happy to be here.

March 14, 2000

Strawberries

Strawberries were not grown commercially in the U. S. until the 1800's because of the abundance of the wild ones. With the development of the Wilson strawberry in 1851, "strawberry fever" swept the country in the 1860's and has not been equaled in intensity by the boom days of any other fruit. The 1909 Census shows Tennessee ranking second in the country with 10,700 acres in strawberry production. Its quick cropping and earliness made it a money maker for many small farmers. It was often shipped up to Northern markets.

For the home fruit garden, strawberries can't be beat. Where tree fruits take many years, the strawberry patch bears its best crop in the second year after planting. By the third or fourth year, production is low, and the patch is rejuvenated or moved. Commercial growers often just get that first crop and then plow them up. A common rotation was strawberries for one or two years; followed by cowpeas (blackeyes, whippoorwills or crowders) planted in June; the following year, vegetables; and the next year, corn with cowpeas between the rows, to be turned under for lots of organic matter for the strawberries to be set into the patch the following spring.

Strawberries love a humus soil, and rotted manure or compost is important for a healthy crop. If fresh manure is used, there will be too many weeds, and a strawberry patch is a little difficult to keep clean anyway. A strawberry plant is fussy about how deep it is set. Get all the roots in the soil, but keep the crown sticking above the ground level. Water them, and they will soon take off.

Blossoms are often pinched off the first year to promote runner formation. The first year runners are the best fruit-bearers for next spring. More compost is spread in August when they are making potential fruit buds. Never fertilize established strawberries in early spring, as this promotes vegetative growth at the expense of fruit production. Mulching is an excellent idea, and pine needles are considered the best mulch. Our patches thrived with them.

There are many different methods of planting strawberries. Hilling, wide row and matting are the most common. They do well in rock gardens or pyramids, and make a wonderful hanging potted plant. Ours are set in a narrow hill, 16 inches apart. A wide row would be a three-foot wide bed with two rows of plants at two-foot centers. Matting is when you set them in a diamond pattern at 14 inch centers. This makes the thickest patch, but it's harder to hoe.

Many varieties are available, but I recommend sticking with what your neighbors are having success with. I like the everbearing variety, Ozark Beauty. Slugs can be a nuisance, and I've heard a saucerful of beer will collect them. The birds deserve a few berries for all the good they do in our gardens with their insect appetites and songs. You'll have no trouble finding ways to eat the berries - jams, cereal, with cream, strawberry-rhubarb pies, wine and, of course, fresh from the patch.

June 1, 1999

Mulberries

Mulberries are a delicious and overlooked fruit belonging on every farm. They grow wild around here, so you may already have these trees. The berry itself is about the size of a blackberry, less tart and softer. It does not hold up well after picking, and I don't know of any commercial mulberry products. Our mulberry pie was delicious, and my neighbor says they also make good preserves.

I planted a handful of Russian mulberry seeds in the late 1970's and kept the 50 foot row free of weeds for a few years. A hedge formed from the trees I didn't sell or give away, and the fruit crop was easy to harvest. They didn't bear well every year, and the trees are precocious. It soon became apparent they were growing too close together, but I was insistent on the hedge idea. They weren't cooperative and kept growing every which way, despite my yearly pruning.

The deer nearly wiped them out about 10 years ago. At this point, I decided to let a tree be a tree, and thinned the mulberries to three trees about 25 feet apart. They have spread out and are as weighted down with fruit right now as I've ever seen them.

Because I planted seed, there is quite a difference in the three trees. The one in the middle bears white mulberries, the only one I've seen like it. The other two are black mulberries, and all three taste sweet, although most people favor the white ones. They seem to have an extra flavor that is quite fruity.

How do you harvest them? Good question. We took a bucket in one hand and ran our fingers up the branch dropping most of them in it. That sure beat picking them one by one. Old sheets were spread out under the tree and the branches shaken. This yielded many berries and not just a few bugs and twigs also.

A bright blue sky illuminated the fan-shaped trees with their unusual leaves. Like a sassafras, mulberry leaves come in three shapes - oval, mitten and three-fingered. Mulberry leaves are a commercial crop in the Orient where they are grown and fed to silkworms, who in turn make fancy silk from the leaves, and I understand it takes a whole lot of leaves to make much silk.

Chapter 5 Berries and Fruit

When I asked an orchardist, "How do you keep birds out of your cherry trees?" he replied, "Plant mulberries". Both are ripe now, at the end of May, but apparently the birds prefer the mulberries and leave the cherries alone. So mulberries are interspersed in cherry orchards. Although many folks haven't tried them, almost everyone who does enjoys a mulberry.

June 1, 1999

Pears

Pears are in, and we are in pears. I eat at least a pair of pears a day, slurpy, juicy ones as sweet as honey. Twenty years ago, I started grafting apple trees. The old-time varieties intrigued me, along with some newer, disease-resistant trees. Soon I had a collection of 70 different kinds of apples, and I started branching out into other fruits. Grapes, berries and pears started appearing around the farm.

Fruit trees are often set out in an open field of grass, and although I have done this often, I don't recommend it. Grass has an inhibiting affect on tree growth. We need to prepare the orchard by liming, plowing, manuring, subsoiling and cover cropping the land well in advance of setting out the trees. I like to look at the orchard as a big garden, and vegetables are a great crop to precede the fruit trees. By cultivating and loosening the soil, composting and mulching, and giving the land the farm's best fertilizer, which is the farmer's own footsteps, the orchard will catch up and surpass one simply planted in a hay field.

"Dig a $10 hole for a $5 tree" is a saying which reflects the importance of thoroughly pulverizing and loosening the soil two feet deep and three to five feet wide for each tree. You'll never get a chance to work the ground again once your tree is planted. Add a few shovelfuls of lime in the bottom of the hole and hit it with the pick a few times. Fill the hole back in with a mixture of compost, good soil and rock dusts.

Set the tree at the same level it was growing at before, with the graft a few inches above ground level. Spread the roots out and bring dirt in all around them. Water it thoroughly and tamp it in with your feet. You may need to protect the trees from rabbits and deer with tree guards and/or fencing.

Ed turned me on to the Magness pear. Ed had tried unsuccessfully for years to raise marketable organic apples and had gone to an Integrated Pest Management program using about 1/3 of the recommended sprays. He told me, "If you want to raise organic fruit, go with pears." I got some twigs from him and grafted a few trees. These were set out in a garden above our vineyard. For several years nothing exciting happened, they just grew and I pruned them and kept the weeds down. One got knocked over when I took a corner too sharp with a round bale of hay behind the tractor.

   The other pear variety, Maxine, had already yielded some nice yellow fruit, but it was the summer of '98 when the Magness pears climaxed. Gushing their luscious fruit, our six trees bore 20 baskets of the sweetest crop I've ever tasted. Unlike most fruits, pears are harvested before they are fully ripe to avoid grittiness. They were kind of green and still crunchy when we picked them on August 19, but in a week they had softened up, and when you put your mouth on a pear, you just suck the whole thing in. We love them to the core. We eat them to the core. We lick the core, wanting more.

   Many of the homesteads around here have an old pear tree or two out back. The big ones are often Bartlett pears and the early, small ones are the June sugar pear. Both can get fireblight, a bacterial infection which turns the ends of the branches black. Wait until winter to prune off the infected branches because summer pruning spreads the problem. When planting a new pear orchard, look for fireblight resistant trees.

   Next to my worm-infested organic apples, the Magness pear is a dream come true. With no disease and very few signs of insect damage, we could sell them for a dollar a pound in Nashville easily. I probably would have, but a light bulb went off in my head. Ed stores his pears in a walk-in cooler, just like the one at the local fruit market. I asked Bo if I could use a corner of the cooler for a few weeks. He said, "Sure, set them in there, I won't be needing the space until we get our fall stuff in." So I did. They would have gone bad fast in this hot autumn weather, but they seem to be keeping well at 38°. We've also put some in the food drier to make dried pears. We'll juice some and can them, too. But mostly I plan on enjoying pairs of pears fresh and juicy while I can.

September 8, 1998

Apples

It won't be long now till it's time to start grafting. February is the month when I graft apple trees. Everyone loves apples, and homegrown apples have so much more flavor than the pretty, picture-perfect supermarket varieties. At the turn of the century, there were over 6,000 varieties of apples. Now there are about 2,000. During the 1700's and 1800's, settlers planted a lot of apple seeds. They grafted from the trees that bore the best fruit and named them, too, so each part of the country had trees that were adapted to that area.

We have had dozens of different varieties of apples on our farm, and it is amazing how unique they all are. Early in July, Lodi, Yellow Transparent and Early Harvest come in with soft apples which are best for pies and sauces. A little later comes one of our very favorites, the Little Strawberry apple that C.H. Hire from Hayesville had growing. His dad had grafted it many years ago, and before the old tree died, we got some twigs, grafted them, and now have this delicious apple that bears for over a month. It's a great apple for eating fresh and can be fried with the peeling on. Towards the end of July, a rich yellow apple, the Golden Sweet, gets ripe. We also have a similar apple called Pink Sweet that we found growing on a farm in Kentucky.

The Grimes Golden is a spicy-flavored, speckled apple that many people may already be familiar with. We have found it to be susceptible to cedar-apple rust, though, which causes orange spots on the leaves. Did you ever notice bright orange, jelly-like fingers from galls on cedar trees after a rain in the spring? Those are the beginnings of the cedar-apple rust that also bothers apples. Luckily, many varieties are resistant to it, and our experimental organic orchard is just the place to learn which ones are and aren't. Because we don't spray, varieties which are susceptible to diseases are obvious and have been culled.

In August, in comes Mollies Delicious, a huge apple shaped like a Red Delicious. With just the right fragrance and texture, it was one of our most popular apples this summer. It's a newer variety, as is Liberty, which I can't say enough good things about. Developed from a Macintosh strain at Purdue University in Indiana, Liberty is resistant to scab, mildew, rust and fireblight and it also tastes great. Crunchy, juicy, tart . . . my mouth waters just thinking about them.

September is really the apple month. Winesaps, like the one out on the Bethany road, soak your chin with their tangy juice. King David, a cross between Jonathan and Arkansas Black, took a long time to bear but was well worth the wait. New varieties like Jonagold, Jonagrimes, Gala and Blushing Golden have fine textures and quite distinctive flavors. The old Rusty Coat has an almost pear-like consistency and is relatively disease-free. I could also mention a dud. Our Black Ben Davis is hard, sour and dry. One of my friends liked it, but there is no accounting for taste. The original Ben Davis is very easy to grow in the South and was shipped up north by the boxcar loads in the 1800's. It was said you could move them with scoop shovels and not bruise the apples.

Fuji is a sweet, crisp apple that does well here and stores great. Half the orchards in Japan are planted with Fuji apples. The Yates apple from Georgia is very small, but packs a flavorful wallop. It has a little bit of red in the flesh and stores very well. It seems odd that the Yates tree here on our farm didn't do well, but the one we planted at Steve and Sally's, which is a graft from our tree, is doing great. It has a better view. I've learned that apple trees like a good view, or maybe it's all the sunshine, good air, and drainage that come from being up on a hill. Dark, dark red with a sweet yellow flesh, Arkansas Blacks have been eaten and fried in these parts for generations. They will keep in our root cellar, hard as rocks till next May, when I might sneak up the hill to eat an unripe early-summer apple. This area is still so very rich in apple varieties that were carefully developed by our ancestors. But as the older trees die out, so will the varieties that are best suited to grow here in Macon County and in this area of Tennessee. If there's anyone out there with an old variety they'd like to see saved, let me know. With a shoot of last year's growth, about the thickness of a pencil, another tree of that variety can someday bear apples just like the original.

January 25, 1994

Pruning

When do you prune fruit trees? When the pruning shears are sharp. For years, I only pruned my trees during the dormant season, usually in late winter. Every summer, the places where I had cut would grow back sprouts that I would dutifully remove the next winter. I was growing apple trees, but not many apples. Now I understand the importance of summer pruning.

Apple trees produce fruit on fruit buds they have made the year before. But they don't make fruit buds if the trees are growing too vigorously. I guess the tree's mechanism is such that when there is plenty of growth going on, they don't feel the need to reproduce by making fruit. Winter pruning stimulates vegetative growth at the expense of fruit bud formation. So now I limit winter pruning to removing damaged limbs and thinning out larger branches. Then in late May or early June, after the first flush of growth, I go through the orchard and prune off the young shoots which I would remove later anyway. Nip 'em in the bud, so to speak. This shocks the tree into forming fruit buds to insure the survival of the species. In short, winter prune to shape the tree and for growing branches, and summer prune for fruit bud production.

There are three types of pruning cuts:

1) removal of larger limbs.
2) thinning cuts, where a small limb attached to a larger limb is removed.
3) heading cuts, where a limb is cut somewhere between the tip and where it connects to the rest of the tree.

I don't use heading cuts anymore. I have found that a branch that needs a heading cut, because it is too vigorous or in the wrong place, just simply needs to be removed.

An easy rule for pruning is to take out any limb that is more than 1/3 the diameter of the branch or trunk where it connects. This gets rid of the more upright vigorous growth and allows the leader, the central trunk, to remain dominant. For example, if your trunk is three inches in diameter, prune off the branches that are more than an inch in diameter. The same holds true for the scaffold branches, those first three or four branches that form the shape of the tree. Look at them as smaller trunks and follow the same plan, also removing any branches that go straight up or down.

Crossing branches should be removed, and the tree should be shaped like a cone, with the lower branches longer and more spread out.

Sometimes I tie down the first branches when the trees are young to help the tree get a wide, spreading scaffold. Remove any branches that come out at a steep upright angle. They will never spread out and will be weak later on. A 45 degree angle or greater is better, as it allows more sunlight to penetrate the tree to ripen the fruit. The cuts should be made close to the trunk or scaffold branches, leaving no stub, but not so flush that it cuts off the little collar that swells where the branch comes out. That should be left, as it has the tree's healing mechanisms in it. No wound dressing is necessary. On larger unpruned trees, don't prune off more than 1/4 to 1/3 of the tree in a single year. It may take a few years to bring them back into the shape you want them. It took me awhile to understand that those big beautiful branches need to come out. It is the smaller spindlier branches that will make fruit buds.

If you nick the bark above a bud, you can sometimes force an otherwise dormant bud to make a branch. By nicking below a bud, a fruit bud is formed. The tips of branches have auxins and hormones in them that regulate reproduction and growth. As sap rises, a bud will sprout a branch if the sap can't rise any higher because of a nick. As the sap descends, the bud above a nick will freak out and want to bear fruit. Isn't nature awesome? By pruning a little now, you can save a lot of work later and stimulate fruit bud formation for next year.

May 2, 1994

Grafting

Grafting fruit trees is an ancient and easy-to-learn art. The Romans were grafting apples long ago, and there are 1,000-year-old grafted chestnuts in Corsica. Most of our modern tree fruits are from grafted, or budded, trees. Ever wonder why people graft trees? The apples, peaches, pears, plums and citrus fruits we love so much are actually mutants. They are deformities in nature. The seeds from these fruits will sprout, grow and make nice trees. But the fruit from these trees will likely be like their wild ancestors. An apple seedling, for example, will make small crabapples.

Every now and then, though, a seedling tree will make bigger, better-tasting fruit. The seeds from this tree may be more likely to make trees with bigger fruit, but usually its offspring will revert back to the small, wild fruits. Gardeners had to figure out how to propagate the big-fruited trees. Someone eventually spliced a twig of a good tree onto some roots and made a new tree that was identical to the original good tree. When that happened, the art of grafting was born. Grafting is like cloning. It is reproducing the mother tree by taking a twig, called a "scion," and getting it to grow on another small tree of the same species.

Johnny Appleseed barefooted his way across pioneer America, collecting and planting apple seeds. Most of his trees were just wild apples, but a few were mutants that had bigger apples. Farmers spotted these trees in the fall, and, as grafting was a common skill, used these trees for scion wood for their own orchards. Paul Stark was a nurseryman who foresaw the value in some good-tasting apples. He gave a large sum of money to a farmer for the exclusive rights to propagate and sell trees grafted from one he called "Red Delicious." His son found the original "Yellow Delicious" while hiking in Virginia. Luckily, the exclusive rights only last for a while, and now we can graft any of the older varieties.

The bright green layer under the bark of a tree is called the cambium, and this is where new cells are made. The new growth on a tree is like the annual growth of smaller herbaceous plants, and the cambium is like a root connecting the new shoots to the tree's roots. If we cut a root and a scion and tape them together so that their cambium layers are touching, they will grow together and make a new tree.

To make a graft, first I get out the old Arkansas whetstone and get my knife razor sharp. After taping up my thumb, I cut a rootstock at an angle a few inches above the roots, exposing about an inch of the inner bark. This cut needs to be perfectly smooth. Then I make a vertical slit down the center of the first cut. The scion wood is prepared the same way, and the two are put together with the vertical slits interlocking. I hold them in place while I wrap the graft with masking tape. The trick is to get the bright green cambium layers to line up. If the root and scion have different diameters, I only line up one side and don't worry about the other. The cells of the cambium layer are the only actively growing part of a tree; this is where the action is. Old-timers used cotton string and beeswax, but I've found masking tape perfect for wrapping the newly grafted tree.

I bundle them in groups of up to 25, then label and store them in a plastic bag at room temperature, with some damp, black sawdust to keep the roots from drying out. They form a callus after about a month, and buds of the scion are swelling and ready to burst if the graft has taken. I line them out in the garden and grow them for a year or two before selling them or setting them out in the orchard.

Budding is similar to grafting, but instead of a twig, just one bud is slipped into an already growing tree. After it has callused, the top of the tree is cut off above the bud. The bud sprouts and grows to make the new tree. If you have an old favorite tree that's on its way out, get me a waterspout of last year's growth, and I'll make you a new tree just like the old one. It's easy, and it's been done for thousands of years.

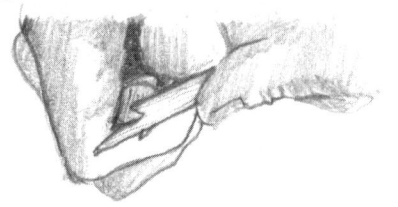

March 7, 1995

Chapter 5 Berries and Fruit

Topworking Fruit Trees

Topworking fruit trees is an old method for changing unproductive or undesirable fruit trees into better ones. Basically, it involves cutting off the limbs of a tree and grafting scion-wood of a different variety onto it. We planted our first orchard in Tennessee in 1974 and added to it the next year. I was interested in old-timey apples, so I bought several trees from a nursery in Georgia which specialized in old varieties. Over the course of a few decades, many of the trees bore fruit, but a couple turned out to be real losers, with small, hard, sour apples that weren't much good for anything. I had read about topworking and decided to give it a try. I was really impressed with the Liberty and Mollies apple varieties in our new orchard, so I got some scion-wood from those trees.

Last year's growth is the best for grafting, so I collected a handful of pencil-sized twigs and headed for the orchard. Good-bye to the Parks Pippen and Shockley as I cut off the major limbs at about head height. First, I made an undercut, so the limb wouldn't tear the bark off the trunk when it fell. Then I cut the limb off and made a smooth surface, about three inches in diameter, on all the branches I wanted to rework. Next, I split the limbs with a wood chisel, not very deep, but enough to pry them open. I then climbed out of the tree and started whittling on the scion-wood. Leaving three or four buds on the scion, I made two sweeping, two-inch long cuts with a razor-sharp grafting knife. The cuts were not parallel, but made a V, so that the scion would fit tightly into the crack in the limbs with the V pointing inwards.

The trick to any grafting is to align the cambium layers - the bright green inner bark where new cells develop - and bind them tightly so that the cells can heal together. Back up in the tree, I pried the crack open with the chisel and inserted two scions into the crack, making certain the cambium layers were touching. After removing the chisel, the scions were snugly in place. Next came the sloppy part. All cut surfaces were covered with pine tar. This excludes air and keeps the scion from drying out while the graft forms a callus. I did this in February when I do all my grafting, and by April, the little buds were opening up. I left one on each limb and cut the other off if both lived.

Some limbs didn't take and had to be topworked again the next year.

This method is called cleft-grafting and will work if the cambium layers make direct contact and don't dry out. Care has to be taken to insure the small shoot gets a chance by removing all other nearby growth. Now I have some funny-looking trees in the orchard with big trunks and limbs which have smaller branches with the new varieties shooting out of them. I prune back any growth from under the new grafts, as that would be more of the old tree. I also took out other branches of the old tree that were left after the new topworked branches got some size on them. I had to leave them for a few years, so the tree would have some big limbs with leaves. I didn't want to kill the tree by removing all of its branches. (This can happen when people top their yard trees too severely, a practice which kills me.)

Sure enough, in a few years the trees started making Liberty and Mollies apples, much better than the old apples these trees had produced. This is how trees are obtained that make more than one kind of fruit - by grafting different kinds to various branches on the same tree. Luther Burbank, a wonderful plant researcher, had 500 different kinds of cherries on one tree! It's amazing the sheer number of fruit varieties that exist, and it's fun to try and grow them. But when one turns out to be a dud, we can make the most of the situation by whacking the top off and utilizing the root system that's already there by topworking a new variety onto it.

December 10, 1996

Persimmons

Persimmons are possibly one of the best things I've ever put in my mouth, and definitely the worst. There is that much difference between a ripe one and an unripe one. Only eat a persimmon if it is soft and the cap comes off easily. Many people think that they need a frost to ripen, but some persimmons are ripe in August and September, and some are never edible. I find persimmon trees mostly on the ridge tops, often along the edge of the woods or alongside a road. It's a small tree with oval leaves which turn a pretty red in the fall. The bark has a distinctive checkered appearance, and the twiggy branches tend to come out horizontally. The inside heartwood is black as ebony, which the persimmon tree is related to. It is used for the fingerboards of homemade stringed instruments, golf clubs, and other products that need a hard, dense wood.

The forestry service often offers persimmon trees by the bundle, at little cost. They seem to think the wood will be valuable in the future. I see the value in the fruit. We may not be able to grow dates or apricots, but at least we have a huge range of different kinds of persimmons. The big, juicy, brown ones ripen first, and soon after are followed by the bright orange ones. One of our orange persimmons is almost seedless. It has a delicate, sweet flavor and is quite moist. Other, darker orange ones are more chewy, like dried fruit. The little black persimmons are almost crystallized sugar. They have a tougher skin, but are very sweet.

Besides being a delicious tropical treat on a cool fall hike, you can gather them up and bring them back to the kitchen. Strain out the skin and seeds. The remaining pulp can be spread out, then dried to make pemmican, a dried persimmon fruit-leather early settlers learned how to make from Native Americans. The pulp can also be added to cornmeal porridge and baked to make persimmon pudding, or try replacing the banana in banana bread with the pulp to make persimmon bread. Cinnamon and nutmeg are good spices to add to persimmon dishes.

The seeds can be washed, roasted and ground to make a delicious coffee substitute, but it does take a bit of work to grind these very hard seeds. Planting the seeds will give you more persimmon trees, but only half of them will bear fruit. This is because some trees are male and others female, with only the female trees bearing the fruit. There are two species of edible persimmons, the native American one, which grows wild around here, and the Asian persimmon, commonly called Kaki. A 1925 gardening encyclopedia lists 14 named varieties of persimmons; early bearing, yellow, orange, red, thin-skinned, large sized, and uniquely flavored ones with a number of other desirable traits. These varieties were grafted onto seedlings and sold in nurseries, so that your persimmon tree will definitely have good fruit. Many other varieties have been found since then, and I am looking for the largest, sweetest persimmons in Macon County.

The Kaki persimmon is Japan's best native fruit. They are grown in Texas, California and Florida. They can get as big as an apple and are very sweet, but I like the flavor of our little wild ones better. Asian persimmons can be firm and crisp or soft and juicy, and some are seedless. They are not as cold hardy as the native persimmon, and cannot stand temperatures much below zero. But in a mild year, they will produce fruit here. I've eaten ripe, homegrown Kakis from Macon County. They are grafted onto the wild persimmon rootstock, and maybe a cold-tolerant variety will be developed one day.

Enjoy some persimmons this fall, but be careful not to eat a hard unripe one. You'll be flying off the hill with a puckered mouth looking for the nearest watering hole.

November 8, 1994

Wine

It's been a grape year. Dry, hot summers really suit the vine and bring out the sugars in the fruit. Rain right before harvest can wreak havoc in the vineyard, especially if you don't spray for black rot. So, although much of the farm suffered from the drought, the grapes thrived. A good hay mulch helped, of course, but mostly to keep the grass and weeds out. Fruits, like other cultivated crops, need to have their spot of ground free of competition. Mulching adds valuable organic matter, conserves moisture, controls weeds and creates a nice soft, soil surface where air can have good access.

Air flow is critical in the vineyard and orchard. We are striving for luscious, sweet fruit, and a lack of fresh air will mean an excess of moisture and, consequently, rot. Eastern exposure is ideal for the early morning sun to dry off the evening's dew. All fruits like a good view, which means up on a hill where the wind blows and the air flows. We grew a cover crop of rye and vetch in a well-composted garden spot and then set out our vines at eight foot intervals.

Manures and compost fertilize the grapes, and over the years we've sprinkled wood ashes and granite meal also. These last two have potash, which helps plants make sugar. Lime is important in the vineyard, as grapes do not like an acid soil. Rock phosphate is beneficial, too. Grapes need severe pruning each spring. Cut back all but 50 or so buds, maybe a dozen or so on four different branches. All fruit is made on the new growth of vines, so just have a trunk and a few short arms, but make sure the wood you're leaving has live buds on it. I neatly pruned a grape plant once only to realize two of the branches I'd left were dead wood. It's alive if it is green when you cut into it.

There are many ways to trellis grapes, a necessary step as they are the "vine". We've used two different methods. Black locust posts were set into the rows eight feet apart. Two rows of wire, at three feet and five feet from ground level, were then stretched on the posts. In another vineyard, we nailed three foot long wooden cross-pieces on five foot posts and ran wires on the ends of them to create a horizontal rather than a vertical trellis, which the vines love, but makes tending underneath them more difficult.

Concord is the easiest variety to grow here. I took cuttings from Ed and Margaret's vines from up at Drapertown back in 1977. They were buried in some old black sawdust for a month to callus and then lined out in the garden for a year before I set them in their permanent home. A grape twig with three or four buds will often form roots if you stick it in the ground with only one bud above the soil level. Delaware and Catawba are other American grapes which will grow here, but the French hybrids are not suited to our climate. The southern part of our county grows great Muscadines, but I haven't had much luck down in the holler with them. I want to try them on top of our highest hill where I fantasize a new vineyard happening someday.

Deer will eat the grapes just as they ripen. We've kept them away with pieces of Irish Spring soap hung on the trellis. To harvest the grapes, I clip the luscious clusters with pruning shears, then sit on the porch and sort through them, placing the good ones in my mouth and in a bowl. After you've filled yourself with grapes, how do you preserve them? Grape jelly and grape juice are good, but the traditional method is wine. All you really need is grapes and water, because they have sugar in the flesh, and grape skins contain yeast. Because I'm using the sweeter Concords (and not the fancy, more disease-prone French wine grapes with unpronounceable names), I add a gallon of warm spring water to four gallons of grapes to make a five-gallon batch of low-alcohol wine.

For a stronger wine, I soak, but don't squeeze, three gallons of grapes in a crock with two gallons of water heated up to dissolve seven and a half pounds of sugar. A packet of Montrachet wine yeast is sprinkled on top after I finish filling up the crock with cold water. You want the water hot enough to completely dissolve the sugar, but no warmer than body temperature when you add the yeast. By just letting them soak and never squeezing the grapes, or any other fruit, the wine is clearer and tastes better. Traditionally, grapes are pressed to make juice and then fermented. Here, we are extracting the juice by soaking and fermenting at the same time.

Chapter 5 Berries and Fruit

To make great wine, keep these tips in mind. Use high quality fruit, only what you would pop in your mouth. Use fresh spring water, never city water or anything but the best water. Use a wine yeast, not bread or beer yeast. Keep all wine equipment very clean. Don't use soap or let the utensils or bottles sit without washing. Wine picks up flavors, so don't use a pickle crock to make wine or you'll end up with vinegar. Light ruins it, so always keep wine in the dark.

After three or four days of soaking in the crock, I gently remove the grapes, or other fruit, with a strainer and pour the liquid into a five-gallon glass carboy. It gets topped off with water and an airlock, which, by means of a water trap, lets carbon dioxide bubble off but no oxygen back in. The carboy is then wrapped with a towel, left to set a couple of months and then racked. Racking is the art of siphoning off the wine with a seven-foot long, three-eighths inch hose to leave the thin layer of yeast at the bottom of the carboy. I let it set a few weeks after racking, and if it's clear, I bottle it and cork it with #9 tapered corks, pressed in with the palm of my hand.

I visited the winery in Jamestown, TN when it first opened and learned a startling fact. Commercial wine has to contain 185ppm of a poison, potassium sulfate, or it is illegal to sell it. Asthma patients are particularly sensitive to this chemical and can't drink store wine. To get good wine, they have to make it. We used the same recipe described above for strawberries, blackberries, raspberries, elderberries, cherries, peaches, plums, pears, apples, blueberries, passion fruit, wild grapes, elderberry flowers, mulberries, and even watermelons and roastin' ears, although these last two I can do without. Wine made with honey instead of sugar is called mead, usually with lemons or some other fruit in it.

Alcohol is an abused substance, so I'm somewhat hesitant to encourage making it. On the other hand, many cultures routinely drink the fermented juice of their beloved vines as part of the preservation of summer's warmth all year long. Homegrown and homemade are often the best you'll ever have.

August 22, 1995

Cider

Variety is the spice of life, and it makes for great apple cider. We like to mix as many different kinds of apples as we can find when we press cider. After gathering the ripe apples on our farm, we hit the back roads of Macon County. Many have apple trees, and many apples just fall and would soon go to waste. These are the ones we're looking for. You can usually tell from the road if the apples under the tree are being gathered and used or not. If it looks like they're just rotting, we bravely pull in the driveway and knock on the door. Explaining that we have an old cider press and are looking for apples to press, we are often invited to clean up all the apples under the tree.

This is a great way to learn about the different apples growing in Macon County, and to meet our neighbors. I've made many good friends this way, returning yearly to see how the trees and people are doing. Once a man met me with a shotgun behind his back, but he mellowed out after we started talking, and now he misses us if we don't show up in the fall. With permission, we'll shake the tree and all the ripe apples will fall. Filling up the bags and our tummies, we load up the truck and head to the press. The apples are sorted and hosed off in milk crates, the bigger apples are kept for pies and sauce. Then the others are loaded in the hopper and the wheels start spinning.

My friend Steve bought the 1869 press at the Doc Kirby place auction for twelve dollars and, with our friend Chris, rebuilt the wooden parts. It's a real beauty, and we can press out a bushel of apples at a time, making about three gallons of cider. The hand-crank turns a huge flywheel and crushes the apples. When the slatted barrel underneath is full, it is pushed ahead under the press, and the other barrel is put under the grinder so we can grind and press at the same time. A round block of wood is placed on the apple pulp and a giant screwpress squeezes downward, releasing gallons of the golden fluid. Pots collecting the juice quickly fill up, and then it's poured through a strainer into jugs. Slipping a glass under the spigot, we all share the sweet nectar, which encourages us to keep washing, grinding and squeezing. It's old-fashioned and fun, and we have a blast, especially if there is plenty of help around.

Afterwards, we clean the press thoroughly, getting every little piece of apple out from between the slats and the grinder. We often hose down ourselves, too. Everyone gets a jug of cider, and we try to take some to the folks who donated the apples. The rest is taken home and canned. We heat it up and pour it into half-gallon jars, seal them, and water bath them for 30 minutes. The juice will keep this way for several years. We feed the dry pumice to the cows, who love it.

We usually do 30 to 40 gallons at a pressing in two or three hours, but yesterday we pressed over 60 gallons. Four families got juice to can and freeze, with lots left over for friends. The only cost is driving around beautiful Macon County making friends and learning about apples. Red and Yellow Delicious are the most common apples here and make a sweet cider. Winesaps are the juiciest, and their tartness adds a great flavor to the mix. The many old-fashioned varieties add different flavors, and it's always exciting to share a new batch of fresh apple cider.

September 5, 1995

White Oak

Fagaceae

Quercus alba

CHAPTER VI

Fields and Farmyard

Cows	147
Fencing	149
My New Love	151
Cheese	153
Hay	155
Corn	157
Wheat	161
Chickens	164
Bees	166
Orchard Mason Bees	169
Insects	171
The Food Web	173

"I have always found what farmers and peasants thought about things much more intelligent than what scientists thought."

Rudolph Steiner

Cows

Cows are a common sight around here, giving a certain warmth to the landscape. Their serene, contemplative chewing of the cud, the frisky playing of the calves, and their economic importance all make me glad to see these animals on the rolling pastures. There is a certain spiritual aspect about them. We've all heard the sayings, "holy cow" or "sacred cow." Farmers need livestock, which includes cows, horses, pigs, sheep, goats and poultry, on their farms to keep the soil fertile. No amount of artificial fertilizers can impart to the soil the life-giving properties of farmyard manure.

In a number of cultures, the cow is a sacred animal. It seems ironic to us that in India people are starving, yet they won't kill a cow. But these ancient cultures knew of the magical properties of cattle. That magic is the cow's stomach. Most animals - and humans, too - have an intestinal tract four or five times as long as their body. It's different for each species and individual. For example, we have about 20 to 30 feet of intestines, but the length of a cow's intestines is 12 times the length of its body, often more than 100 feet. In this extra digestive system, an amazing process takes place. From the four stomachs of a cow, grass and other foods are coughed back up for the cow to chew again. Of course, this sounds gross to us as we recall the very unpleasant taste of regurgitated food, but the peaceful expression on a cow's face as it is chewing its cud belies a different experience.

As the cow is leisurely enjoying its cud, the grass is being turned not only into cow food, but food for the soil that grew the cow's meal. What comes out at the end of the cow's digestive process is the finest soil-enhancing material. It points to an important but often overlooked phenomenon. The annual dropping of manure from a cow, properly handled, can make about four acres of land fertile, while the same cow can live off approximately two acres. It is this ability of the cow to give more than it receives that makes her so valuable. It's true that a cow doesn't have the intelligence of a horse or offer the companionship of a dog, but with their stomachs, they fulfill a necessary niche on our farms. With the cows we keep on our small farms today, we ensure the health of the farms for tomorrow. Where farming is done without animals in the cycle, soil life suffers.

Ultimately, a dependency on more and more artificial fertilizers leads to the necessity of pesticides, fungicides and herbicides, furthering the decline in the health of the soil and environment, hence the quality of the food and the health of humans. On the other extreme, huge feed lots with cattle, fed on imported grain, produce massive amounts of manure. This is regarded as a waste product since it is too far to truck it back to the cornfields. Pasture is the natural food for cattle, and they should be allowed to roam about picking at a variety of plants. They know what's good for them. Years of huge buffalo herds roaming the plains - eating, stomping, pooping, then moving on for many moons before returning - is what created the black, fertile cornbelt land of the Midwest. This relative of the cow was rightfully held sacred by Native Americans.

A particularly good idea is rotating pastures often during the year, letting the herd completely graze down a nice 6 to 12 inch tall stand of forage and then moving them to a fresh pasture. That way the grazed and manured plants can recover and spring back up, and the cattle are always eating the lushest growth. Keeping them in one lot tends to pack the ground. It also creates an overgrazed pasture part of the time and an undergrazed pasture during the peak growing season. It is better to have a bunch of cows in small lots for short periods of time rather than letting them have free range of the whole farm all year.

The warm earthy colors of cattle munching on green pastures is a picture we have had with us since the dawn of civilization. Shepherds moved their herds around daily, rotating pastures instinctively to maintain healthy flocks and good soil fertility. They knew the detrimental effects of over-grazing or of not having any animals on the land. Domesticated animals have played an integral part in humanity's religions, evolution and daily bread. Holy Cow!

December 27, 1994

Chapter 6 Fields and Farmyard

Fencing

Whoever invented barbed wire must have had a mean streak, I was thinking, as we strung up a mile of it last week. I'd never used a tractor-driven posthole digger before, and since it was borrowed, I was pretty sure I'd tear it up. But after figuring out how to mount it, I was again impressed by modern work-saving devices. Fifteen holes in less than an hour, and I was well on the way to a new pasture. The Solstice field runs next to the creek (or vice-versa), and I'd wanted to fence it in for a few years. I wanted cow manure in the field, but not in the creek, so I needed a fence.

I kept putting it off because the landscape was so pretty, and I didn't want to ruin the view with barbed wire. But many factors finally motivated me, not the least of which was that I'd run out of hay. Corner posts were set in deep with braces, and I used sycamore and box elder trees along the way. Every 20 paces got a locust or cedar post if a tree wasn't handy. Tamping rocks in with a big iron bar to get the post tight is a good workout. After years of unwinding barbed wire by using a stick through the roll, with it spinning uncomfortably close to my hands, someone told me about a spinner they sell at the Co-op. It costs six bucks, and the wire rolls off much safer and easier. I've tightened barbed wire with come-alongs, the tractor, and various other strong-arm tactics, but, personally, I prefer the two-hammer method. I grab the barb with the claw of a hammer and pull against the post while my other arm (or partner) nails the staple in. Not super tight, but good enough for me. I can't handle too much tension.

It was a beautiful day to be outside, bright blue sky with puffy clouds rolling by, and we philosophized as we went from tree to tree, post to post. By the next day, we had the wire up and started pounding in metal posts about every four paces. All the while the cows, who think the sound of an engine is the dinner bell, were quite interested in our project. We opened the gate and poured some corn in their new pasture. It took a few minutes, as cattle are shy about new things. The only other times they were out there, they weren't supposed to be, and I had let them know it. But Red-Eye carefully wandered out, followed by Jenny, and soon they were all happily munching the little

Chapter 6 Fields and Farmyard

bit of fescue this bottomland had on it. That left us to fix a gap, which was just a barbed wire opening, to get in and out of the field.

This land was calling for cattle, just as they were needing the grass. I cut hay here every year, but hadn't manured it, and it wasn't long till my plan was working. I'll leave the cows in this field for a couple of weeks and then turn them back into their summer pasture. The hay should do better after having the cattle here. Besides their manure, the meadow will benefit from the animal impact of cow hooves digging around, as well as that lovely cow breath full of the carbon dioxide that plants live on. I'll turn them back in here for a week or two after I cut the hay, too. Both the land and the cows will be happier.

A fellow from India visited us last week, and I asked him about his cattle farm. He said they use thorny plants in hedges to fence cows in. They use the oxen for draft animals, make dairy products, and use cow manure for fertilizer and fuel, but they don't kill them. We have wild rose, hedge apple, locust, autumn olive, green briar, blackberry, wild plum, and many other thorny hedge plants here on our farm. I guess if we'd been farming here for a few thousand years and didn't have barbed wire, we'd also have natural thorny hedges around our fields.

March 21, 1995

My New Love

The early morning sun finds me on a knoll overlooking the Long Hungry Creek to the east and the Sugar Camp waterfall reflecting the light back from the west. This is where we've built a small milking shed, and this is where Annie and I rendezvous. She is always glad to see me. I think she has a crush on me, but Deb says it's my corn. The corn is crushed.

I traded some of our calves for four Jersey milk cows last fall, and Millie was the first to freshen. But she liked being with her calf more than the milking routine, which included being separated from him all night, so I just let them be after a few mournful mornings of mooing madness. I had toyed with the idea of selling milk this spring. Several of my friends who like milk would rather not take chances with commercial milk. But I don't have a refrigerator and have plenty to do besides washing milk jars. I also had discovered that selling whole milk is illegal except for use as pet food. At one time, we got $3 a gallon for the milk (with the cream) and $2 a quart for yogurt. Years ago, it was common for most people around here to get their dairy products from their farms or their neighbors. It was a way to make a few bucks, get good food locally, and create soil fertility.

I had about given up the idea of milking at all when Deb came back from her pasture hike with the news. The new cow with the dishpan face was bawling over her dead calf. Coyotes or dogs had already gotten there and may have been the culprits. Annie Belle Lee let us milk her in the pasture right away. We did not use the colostrum milk, a cow's first few yellowish-colored milkings, essential for the newborn calf. Next morning, I went to the pasture and hooted, and she came running. I rubbed her sack and she eased into the milking position.

I use two methods for milking. With my thumb and first finger, I cut off the milk in the teat from the udder, then successively squeeze my other three fingers and squirt the milk out. I claim this is good practice for guitar playing. After this gets boring, I alternate to the two finger method, which is actually my thumb and first two fingers that I slide up and down on a teat. This method is good for stripping out the last of the milk so that the cow doesn't get mastitis.

Chapter 6 Fields and Farmyard

Back at the house, I want to strain the milk through a milk filter into wide-mouth gallon jars, but had run out of filters. I can't find them in Macon County, as our Co-op quit stocking dairy supplies, because we don't have dairies around here anymore. So until I can get to Tompkinsville, I'm using a T-shirt. The milk then goes to the root cellar, which at this time of year is quite cool. The next morning finds a pint and a half of cream floating on the milk. Quickly ladled into a jar and shaken up, the magic of butter congeals and separates from the buttermilk, which we strain off and use for biscuits. A gallon of the skim milk was warmed up to 185 degrees and 1/4 cup of apple cider vinegar was stirred in, and we strained out our first cheese for dinner. More milk was scalded and then cooled to body temperature. To a quart of this, we stirred in a tablespoon of yogurt, wrapped the jar in a blanket to insulate it, and eight hours later we had a quart of yogurt. Custard out of home-grown milk, honey, and eggs is another treat (don't forget the vanilla), as is cream for the coffee, and, best of all, milk for my favorite meal, cornbread and milk. Farm life is the good life.

Back in the pasture, Dishpan Annie is number one cow, the only cow who gets a few minutes with her head in a feed bucket every day, which makes the other cows jealous. I am truly enjoying the morning chore with Annie, but if the newness wears off and I get tired of it, I'll get her some calves to adopt. Jersey cows can raise several calves a year with their rich and plentiful milk. But for now, I appreciate waking up with her and all the treats her teats bring to the table. The farm has become more productive, and, if I fatten up a little, maybe I won't be so long and hungry.

March 4, 1996

Cheese

Homemade cheese is back in style here at our wood-fired "Cafe." A new recipe for a mozzarella-type string cheese is so delicious we are compelled to share it, along with our old farmers and Riccota ones.

First, we ladle the cream off a few days' milkings to get two gallons of skimmed milk. Two and one-half teaspoons of citric acid powder is dissolved in 1/4 of cup water and mixed into the milk until completely dissolved, about two minutes. The milk is in a large stainless steel pot and now gets warmed up to 98 degrees. Liquid rennet is mixed into 1/4 cup cold water and stirred into the milk for 1/2 minute. Rennet coagulates milk in 30 minutes to an hour. It turns milk into curds and whey. Rennet is made from the stomach lining of a calf, although the rennet we bought is a new substitute made from vegetables. It sure works to form a big white lump floating in a pot of whey.

Did you ever wonder how cheese-making was discovered? A long time ago people milked cows and goats, but there were no handy jugs to carry the milk in. What did they use instead? Any possible container was utilized, from crockery to gourds to the stomach linings of animals they'd slaughtered. One day, when the prodigal son returned home, the father of the house killed a calf to celebrate. A younger son, named Cheese, had to go milk and, as all the gourds and crocks were being used at the feast, he grabbed the calf's stomach lining and poured the milk into it. Lo and behold, a few hours later it had turned to curds and whey, and he gave it to little Miss Muffet.

The next step is to cut the curd into 1/2-inch cubes, crisscrossing the top and slicing at an angle to get them all small enough. They sit for five minutes and then are put back on the low heat part of the wood cookstove, where they slowly warm up to 108 degrees. This takes about 20 minutes, stirring gently, and then continue to stir another 20 minutes after you remove them from the heat. Now it's time to separate the curds from the whey by pouring them through a colander. Adding a little salt to the curds produces a delicious farmer's cheese.

The whey can be used to make Riccota cheese by adding a pint of milk, heating to 200 degrees and stirring in 1/4 cup of apple cider vinegar. Ricotta cheese will appear and can be scooped up with a strainer.

The mozzarella method is to cut the curd into one-inch strips and lay them in a bowl; add 1/2 cup salt to a gallon of water heated to 170 degrees and pour on the curds. Underwater in the bowl, stretch the curds like you would pull taffy. They get stringy and shiny, and after 10 minutes, can be kneaded on a board like bread. Roll the cheese up in a ball and soak in cold water to stiffen it up. To store it, just dry it with a towel, wrap it in a plastic bag and refrigerate. It can also be stored in the cold water. Unlike the farmers cheese we make, this cheese melts when baked, so is great for casseroles, pizzas and omelettes. It's a wonderful way to use up the extra milk that Annie gives us every day. Hard cheeses are made by pressing the drained curds instead of stretching them. After they are thoroughly dried and pressed, the block of cheese is dipped in wax and aged for a month or two.

To make a stronger, whangy-flavored cheese, allow the milk to sour a little bit by adding some yogurt to it and letting it set for a few hours. The size you cut the curds into also determines the kind of cheese: cheddar is made by cutting the curds into 1/4 inch cubes, American, 1/2-inch cubes, and Muenster is cut into 3/4-inch cubes. Along with the unique flavors of different yogurt cultures, cheeses are further enhanced by aging. But our new string cheese doesn't require aging. If it wasn't so good, maybe we would try aging it.

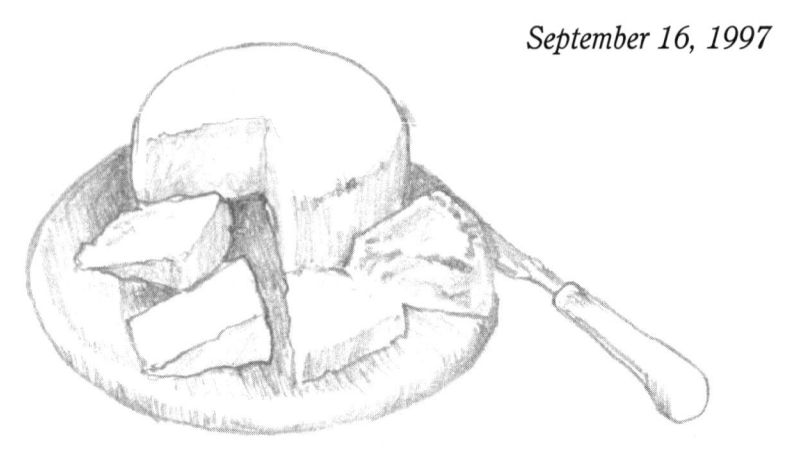

September 16, 1997

Chapter 6 Fields and Farmyard

Hay

Cutting hay makes me a little nervous. There are so many sharp, hard metal things moving so fast. But it needs to be done, so I grease up the sicklebar mower and take inventory of the spare parts I ought to have on hand, such as extra guards and bolts, blades and rivets, and a pitman stick. Then I throw a few appropriate tools in the box and fill the tank with gas.

The outside row has many branches down from last winter's ice storm. I'll drive across them with the sickle bar pointing in and get the outside swath after I finish the field. I love it when the machinery runs like a sewing machine, crisp and clean, laying down the fescue, clover and miscellaneous weeds. I imagine the weeds are herbs that benefit the cattle to some extent, like adding herbs and spices to our food. The diversity is bound to be healthful for both the land and the animals.

The mower started binding up on a certain guard, so I checked it and found it needed replacing. Binding up happens quite a bit because picking rocks out of the hayfields is low on the list of things to do this time of year. I figured I'd do it last winter, but I haven't yet, so I'll be replacing a few blades and guards. It's amazing how aware I become of every little sound as I make the ever-decreasing rounds, knowing I can save myself trouble by listening for potential problems.

There are a lot of tricks to mowing hay. Turning corners quickly, getting that last sliver of hay without picking up what's already been cut, jumping over rocks and low places, and avoiding the ever-frustrating bind so I don't have to shut the PTO off, get off the tractor, and pull the hay out to see what's going on. As the teeth slip through the grass, and certain places aren't cutting as well as they could, I've learned that by filing a blade or tightening a guard, I can avoid bigger troubles later on. Actually, the whole hay mowing, raking, baling process is one big hassle after another, even without thunderstorms threatening to ruin it all, which are common at haying time. But it is an integral part of the whole farm operation, maybe the most important, because hay crops improve the structure of the soil.

Cutting off the tops of the plants is accompanied by the roots dying back, which, in turn, decay and create topsoil. The regrowth of the hay uses this new humus, and the process repeats. (I figure this is why Americans like a freshly mown lawn, which is in a continual humus production process from the growing and mowing. There is an instinctual part of us that wants to be around good soils.) Also, of course, the hay will be fed to the farm animals, and their manure is the key to the fertility of the farm.

Our hay was thin this year. It makes cutting easier (always look for the bright side), but I'd thought with all the rain in April, it would have been thicker. I only have 25 acres in hay, but it takes a while to mow as there are eight different fields with little dabs of hay separated by creeks, hills and woods, so I need to lift up the bar between each field. This requires attention, because the sickle can slip down as I lift, and I need to know where my fingers are if I want to keep them. All my digits are relieved when this job is over.

So I've spiraled around the farm like a Tasmanian devil, not even stopping for a fresh green salad. It's highly unlike me to pass up food, but I get a different kind of nourishment smelling the wild roses on each round in the field and enjoying the view from up on the hill. From the top, I have a clearer picture of the overall health of the farm, from weaker areas which need composting to spotting other chores like summer pruning the new orchard. Things to do appear as I circle round and round.

The cows munching spring pastures seem oblivious to all I go through for them. Over in the corner is a compost pile from last year's hay feeding, and the fields have fertility from previous years of haying and feeding cows. The farm feels whole and quite interrelated. With a stiff neck and a sore rear end (I'm buying a new tractor seat tomorrow), I gaze out on acres of lawn, breathe in the aroma of new mown hay, relax and let the earthworms turn the dying roots and unraked spots into topsoil. I take off my shoes and start hoeing corn.

May 31, 1994

Corn

Corn is a magical plant and a double-edged sword. A delicious food and a fast, easy-to-grow grain integral to our small farms, it is also responsible for some of the worst soil erosion I've seen in Tennessee. Field corn endeared itself to me when I was a teenager trying to break an Appaloosa colt. I would always have a pocket full of kernels, and Sweetheart would follow me everywhere on the farm. (My propensity to leave a few corn seeds in every chair I sat in, along with my voracious appetite for cornbread, earned me the nickname Corn Boy.)

I was growing Trucker's Favorite back then, a white dent corn that grew huge plants with large ears, often over a foot long. Now I have a cross of several old kinds, resulting in a wide variety of colorful ears. Having a stash of corn in the barn or a corn crib definitely makes you popular around the barnyard. From chickens to pigs, goats, horses and cows - they all love corn. Corn is a grass like all the other grain crops. Its bushy roots and long, pointed, sharp leaves indicate that it is a silica plant, a monocotyledon, contrasting with the deep tap roots and round, softer leaves of the calcium-loving legumes, which are dicotyledons. So corn often follows beans in crop rotations. It loves the extra nitrogen where the beans have grown.

I grew up on a 40 acre diversified family farm in Illinois, and then we moved to a 300 acre corn and soybean farm when I was 12. Dad retired and became a devout organic gardener, but he leased out the fields to our neighbor, who farmed with the latest in agricultural technology. This meant plowing from fence row to fence row, no animals, many chemicals and huge equipment. It didn't take Dad long to put two and two together. A small farm organism, producing its own feed, fertilizer and food, only makes a profit for the farmer. The agribusiness corporations sought to undermine this self-sufficiency with a growing dependence on the products they sold. They funded land-grant colleges, whose research, of course, echoed their advertising.

During the five and a half years I lived there, we saw a noticeable decline in wildlife and birds, trees dying and terrible ground water pollution. Huge drifts of topsoil piled up when the wind blew. Earthworms can't live in these dead soils, but they thrived in Dad's organic garden. Soil erosion is greater now than in the Depression years, with 5 to 20 tons of topsoil lost for every ton of grain produced. The sand underneath this wonderful black soil is getting closer to the surface yearly.

Dad joined the Farmer's Union and was visiting the neighbors trying to get an alfalfa mill put in so a healthy cover crop could be profitably grown. He learned that not long before, all the farms there were small farm organisms, complete with cattle, pigs, chickens, gardens, orchards, hay fields, pastures, wetlands and woods. Dad would get so upset when the Secretary of Agriculture would warn farmers to "get big or get out," advising them to cut down trees, remove fences and plow up as much land as they could. The banks lent large amounts of money to farmers so they could buy bigger tractors, always a farmer's dream. (I still suffer from this myself.) Each spring, hundreds of thousands of dollars were borrowed, and thousands of acres were fertilized, planted, sprayed and harvested. The corn and soybeans were then taken to the elevator, and the farmer had two choices: sell at the current price or rent elevator space in hopes that the prices would rise. The price of grain fluctuates on what is called the commodity market. Businessmen buy the grain "futures" at a low price and sell at a high one. Much money is made this way, at the farmer's expense. So at the end of the year, the farmer pays his bank back with interest, supports a few faraway businessmen, has no time for a garden and, if he's lucky, breaks even. All the while, more and more chemicals are applied each year and most of the corn is used for cattle feed thousands of miles away.

The ancestors of our corn were the staple food of many Native American people. Columbus was the first to bring corn back to Europe, where it quickly gained popularity. The Old World grains - wheat, rye, barley and oats - are all much smaller seeds that are more difficult to harvest. They need to be cut, shocked, dried, threshed, hulled and winnowed (all done with a combine now), while each ear of corn is already a handful of food. We let corn dry in the barn loft, shuck it, and then run it through a corn sheller. When its moisture content is below 14%, it is ready to grind into meal. Edwin and Velma have an old stone grist mill on their farm. Edwin and their son, Billy, crank up the ancient, one-cylinder John Deere engine, and soon we all have warm meal on our chins and noses as we taste the freshly ground corn. Velma is quick to get a hoecake on the griddle so we don't bloat on raw corn meal. Hoecakes are a delicious stove-top version of cornbread.

This is the cornbread recipe I use:

First, preheat the oven to 375 and put a cast iron skillet on a low flame.

Then mix two cups of corn meal with one cup of whole wheat flour (or substitute spelt or unbleached flour) with a rounded teaspoon of soda and a pinch of salt.

Stir it well, then create a well and crack an egg into it.

Beat this up, then add two Tbsp. honey (which reacts with the soda to make the bread rise) and enough liquid (water, milk, buttermilk, soymilk or sour milk) to make a loose batter.

Next add two Tbsp. oil and stir well.

Drop about a tablespoon of oil into the hot skillet, then pour the mixture into it and let it stay on top of the stove for a minute. Put the skillet into the oven for around 30 minutes or until the top is golden brown.

After it's cooled for a few minutes, I eat a slice with butter or in a bowl with milk. A hoecake is smaller, left to cook on the griddle, and flipped over like a big pancake. Better eating is hard to find, unless you're making hominy.

To make hominy, I soak a few cups of corn with a few tablespoons of baking soda overnight, then drain and rinse them before they are set on the stove to simmer for a few hours. When the kernels pop open and the hulls loosen, I work them with my hands like I'm kneading dough to remove the husks, which float away in the rinse water. Then I run the kernels through a grain mill. The hominy is then ready to eat, with a little salt or molasses. It can be made into patties or rolled out on a flour board to make Mexican tortillas, quickly fried on a hot griddle.

Yes, I love corn, but my farm has definitely suffered from it. The Old World small grain crops are grown close together and not cultivated, so soil erosion is not a big problem with them. But corn is grown in rows three feet apart with plants a foot apart in the row, and all this bare ground in between is subject to erosion and the ill effects of tillage. It can wash away when it rains. And it did. All the farms where corn was grown on sloped land suffered immensely during the earlier years of agriculture. You can see the gullies in pastures that were once corn patches.

So we need to be careful with this sacred plant of the Americas. I can hardly see farming without it, but it has ruined many a good farm. But corn can also be a great soil improver. Look at all the organic matter in a corn field in July and August when it's shooting up so fast you can almost hear it growing. If it is all taken off for silage and no manure returned, the soil will be greatly depleted. But if it is mowed and disced in at that time, the soil gets a great green manure crop.

December 6, 1994

Wheat

Growing wheat may be the oldest form of agriculture, as it was one of the first plants to be domesticated in ancient civilizations. Our attempt to grow our own food has to include wheat, because grains are so important in the diet; bread is the staff of life. In October, a composted garden spot is rebroke with a chisel plow and harrow. Seed is rhythmically tossed out from a bucket as we walk over the field and then we harrow it in. That's it until harvest time.

There are two types of wheat - soft and hard. The soft wheat is what's mostly grown here in Tennessee. It is used for animal feed and as pastry flour for baking. Hard winter wheat has higher protein and gluten (that's the gooey stuff that makes bread rise) and is grown in the more fertile Great Plains States. It is the best for bread, so we grow it instead of the soft wheat. Wheat is sometimes grown as a cover crop, too, instead of rye. It can be pastured in the spring, and then the ground used for tobacco or other row crops. Our gardens are pretty fertile, so a light dressing of compost and rock phosphate seems to adequately fertilize the wheat crop. Its lush green leaves make a beautiful cover in the fall, and it starts growing again early in the spring. When it's about a foot tall, I undersow with white clover, so that after harvest there will be a stand of clover on the field.

Hairy vetch is one of my favorite cover crops. By late spring, its growth has created much organic matter, and it also adds nitrogen to the soil. The roots help loosen the ground, too. We plant it with rye on most of our tilled land in the fall and believe it really helps with the overall improvement of the farm. I never could understand why my dad didn't like hairy vetch. "That vetch will get out of hand and be a weed," he would say. But the vetch doesn't like to grow in the summer and never was a problem at all, until I started growing wheat. My dad was from Kansas, which is wheat country, and he knew vetch as a weed because it climbs up the wheat, and instead of waves of amber grain, you have spots of purple flowers. I've pulled some vetch out of the wheat field, but it has tendrils and pulls up the wheat. So I've left most of it, and it looks like I'll have a little vetch flour with my wheat flour. It's a legume, so maybe it'll be good for me.

In early June, the kernels of wheat are still milky when you squeeze them. By late June, they are hard and shatter out of the ear, and it's time to harvest the grain. We have an old 1929 combine that we pull behind our tractor. Everything on it rattles and shakes as it cuts the wheat, and the arms that move it onto the belts get clogged way, way, way too often. If I could get the belts tighter, maybe they wouldn't clog so much, but of course all the bolts have 50-plus years of rust on them, and I doubt if I could find another canvas in town. So we keep on truckin' through our 1/2-acre wheat field all afternoon just to get a half dozen bushels of grain for our year's supply of flour. Much of the grain is still in the field when we finish - a gleaner's dream.

Back at the barn, the bags are full and heavy, but still have trash in them. Now it's time to separate the wheat from the chaff. We use an old seed cleaner that came from Amish country and is in quite good shape. You turn a crank with a flywheel, and all sorts of screens start shaking with dust aflying, and out the bottom comes your clean wheat. This process also takes a long time, but it beats winnowing it by pouring the wheat out from the barn loft on a windy day to catch it in a basket to get it clean, like we used to do.

In the house with our prized gold, we light up the cookstove, dissolve some yeast, and pour the grain into our hand-grinding mill. This is the real work. I grind it coarsely, and then run it through again at a tighter setting, sift it, and stir some of it into the warm yeast water with a little honey. After the sponge rises, I stir in the rest of the flour, add some salt and oil, and let it rise again in the warming racks above the stove. By now the oven is hot, and the bread rises one more time in the loaf pans, then into the oven, and the house begins to have that heavenly, fresh-bread aroma.

The difference between homegrown bread and store-bought bread is about the same as the difference between a homegrown tomato and a store-bought one, if not more. So after all our labors, we are now getting our sustenance from this ancient grain that has been with our culture for so long. The seeds are offspring from those first days of agriculture and the very beginning of civilization.

As I march through the autumn fields sowing seed, I may chant a Sanskrit verse or otherwise keep my head relatively clear and focused.

Chapter 6 Fields and Farmyard 163

Each step and toss is like the last one and the next one, and I am almost a machine. I actually have a machine to do this, a grain drill. It has a place for the wheat seed and for the clover seed, and plants them in nice little rows. I've used our hand-crank seeder for wheat, too. But since I've only half an acre to plant, I'd rather commune with my ancestors in this sacred act of sowing grain. It is truly an honor to work the land to get our daily bread, and there is not much I'd rather eat.

July 5, 1994

Chickens

I can't imagine a farm without chickens. Their early morning crowing is our alarm clock, and a couple of eggs gets me started at breakfast. Our first chickens were Rhode Island Reds, and they arrived in the fall of 1975 as day-old chicks. Buff Orpingtons are the big yellow chickens. Domineckers are the black and white striped ones, also called Barred Rocks. There are white and brown Leghorns and many Asian chickens with funny tufts of hair on their feet or heads. Banties make the best moms, but they fly well and are hard to keep in a pen.

Baby chicks are absolutely the cutest little creatures, like fluffy eggs with legs. We called them "peepers," and they were quite lively and curious about the world. They were fed a chick starter and soon were eating henscratch. Chickens love to peck at anything, so we fed them kitchen and garden scraps. We always keep oyster shells available, as they need some grit for their gizzards. Fresh water is also important, and their water was changed daily. By spring, our chicks were chickens and laying an egg every day. We were making laying mash by boiling soybeans for them. Laying mash can be purchased at the feed store.

Chickens should run free, or so we thought. It wasn't long before we realized that chickens and a freshly-planted garden don't mix well. After they repeatedly scratched up our seedlings, we decided to build a chicken pen. Our coop is long and narrow with south windows for winter warmth. We have a dozen nests, and the roost has a dropping pit under it. This is just a box made with 2 x 6 boards with wire over them to collect manure and to keep the chickens from scratching in it. The coop is near the house for easy, daily access, but there wasn't any room to build a pen nearby because of the brook which ran behind the chicken house. So we built a chicken bridge with a wire tunnel 50 feet long on either side and made the chicken run on the other side of the brook. We clip one of their wings if they escape too often from the five-foot tall pen. We mow the pen occasionally, but keep lots of tall stuff around for the chickens to hide underneath when the hawks fly.

We planted mulberries along the fence to drop berries for the chickens to eat, and the trees offer some protection. Predators are a real problem for chickens, and they don't have much of a defense. We saw a rooster attack a hawk once. It lost its life, but it saved the chickens. Possums, foxes and dogs all love to eat chicken, and the eggs are eaten by everything. We routinely find king snakes in the nests and even had to get rid of a cat which kept sneaking into the coop and eating eggs. We shut the coop up every night at dusk.

We save eggshells, bake them, crush them, and give them back to the chickens, recycling some calcium. They will eat their own eggs if they need calcium, so we don't feed them raw eggshells since that might encourage it. One of the more convincing arguments for the biological transmutation of elements is the increase of calcium from an egg to the baby chick. Where did it come from?

Chickens make great pets. When I was seven years old, I had one that followed me wherever I went. We routinely give them names according to their personalities and antics. Our first dog, Queenie, was humiliated by Beauregard, a proud rooster, eating out of her dog bowl, but wouldn't do anything about it because of her lesson in chicken killing. Last year, a black hen escaped, and we figured she was dead. Three weeks later, we found her and her babies hiding in the comfrey patch not six feet away from where we get water daily. Mama Comfrey raised up some lovely hens and is happily back in the coop.

Chickens have an oil gland on their backs, and when preening their feathers, they are actually spreading oil to keep water off their skins. Hens make many different clucking sounds, depending on whether they are finding a worm, bragging on their latest eggs or talking to their chicks. Their rich manure is a welcome addition to the compost pile, and all plants perk up with a drink of chicken manure tea.

One of our friends has a chicken tractor. A portable coop and pen are moved around her garden every few weeks, leaving behind ground that is bug-free, fertilized, scratched up and ready to plant. Chickens and eggs will always have a place on a farm, whichever came first, the chicken, the egg, or the farm.

July 11, 1995

Bees

We have very busy and industrious workers here on our farm. Besides insuring that we have good fruit and vegetable crops, they supply us with an important and unique food. We just extracted three gallons of the most wonderful honey yesterday, from clear white clover honey to beautiful, dark buckwheat honey.

In the Spring of 1975, I ordered a package of bees. We didn't check our mail the day they arrived, but our dedicated postmaster fed them sugar water to keep them alive until we got them. The package of bees is placed in a hive, and the queen is set inside in a separate container. The bees have to eat through some candy to free her, and by this time have made themselves at home. The hive is a stack of square boxes with two different sized frames in them: a deep one on the bottom for the bees to raise their brood in, and shallow ones on top for them to store their honey in.

The queen makes her maiden flight high in the sky, and the drone, or male bee, that can fly the highest mates with her. Then all the males are useless, and the queen lays fertile eggs for the rest of her life. The worker bees are infertile females that only live about 40 days in the summer, literally working themselves to death. They fly from flower to flower gathering nectar. Pollen gets stuck on their legs, and when they go to another flower, the pollen can fall off and fertilize it. Without bees pollinating flowers, we would not have many of our favorite fruits and vegetables.

Once when I left an old abandoned hive outside, wild bees took up in it. These turned out to be the best bees we've ever had, although they were slightly more aggressive than tame bees we'd had before. Then came the mite problem. Varona and tracheal mites are a big worry to bee-keepers now. We lost our hives a few years ago and many others have lost theirs. But last summer an empty hive once again had bees in it, and they have done very well. Overall, I don't see near the number of bees outside that I'd like to see, and this could be a great concern for agriculture.

To harvest the honey, the frames of honey are scraped with a hot knife to remove the wax coating which the bees have sealed it with.

Then the frames are put in a honey extractor, a big cylinder whose insides spin around with a hand crank. The honey flies out to the sides of the cylinder and runs down into the bottom, where it is taken out and put into jars. This method leaves the combs intact so the bees don't have to build the hexagonal, wax storage containers again and can spend more time making honey. We leave plenty of honey in the hive so that they have enough food to get through the winter. Taking the excess off in June gives them plenty of time to make more honey all summer, and also helps to keep them from swarming.

A swarm of bees is a sight to behold. A cloud of buzzing, swirling bees will be flying around the farm, and we bang on a metal lid with a stick. They alight on a tree branch, and we attempt to climb up the tree, cut the branch, and set the clump of bees inside a new hive box. Bees, when swarming, are quite gentle, as they've just gorged themselves with honey and aren't likely to sting. We make use of this trait when we work with bees. I dress up tightly in a bee suit with a screen hat and use a smoker to blow smoke into the hive. The bees, thinking the hive is on fire, gorge themselves with honey in case they need to fly far away and are much more mildly behaved when I look into the hive a few minutes later.

A colony of bees, like that of ants, is an amazing group effort. One queen lays all the eggs and sexless workers do all the work. Males are raised for the one mating and then disposed of. Bees can quickly identify bees from another hive. Robber bees are guilty-looking bees sneaking around weak hives stealing honey. All bees work for the common good of their colony and readily sacrifice their lives for it, as they die soon after using their sting. They communicate with each other by means of their antennae, and the hive as a whole has a remarkable intelligence. If the queen dies, they'll raise another one and keep or kill drones as need be. They have no trouble finding the buckwheat patch we plant for them.

An example of Nature's complex relationships is the honeybee on her excursions gathering nectar from flowers. She will only visit one kind of flower on each trip, apples this time and maybe clover on the next venture, but never apples and clover on the same pollen-gathering flight, thus insuring pollination. A yeast is left behind on the clover plant by the visiting honeybee, and this yeast helps the plant become more digestible to the cows who graze it. The cow's manure is then more valuable to the clover later on.

The study of bees is quite interesting, from watching them talk to each other coming in and out of the hive to hearing them cool the hive in summer by fanning it with their wings, or imagining their mating ritual way up towards the sun. But, best of all, is seeing them work the clover and apple blossoms while we're enjoying our flowers' essence on a warm piece of homemade bread.

June 25, 1996

Orchard Mason Bees

The orchard mason bee could be an answer to our bee problems. Many people have asked me about the mite problem in honeybees and the future of bee-pollinated crops. Long before the honeybee was brought to the New World by the colonists, the orchard mason bee was pollinating fruits here. It is actually a much better springtime pollinator, and is native to all of the United States. This bee is not a hive-dwelling, social bee. It lays eggs in a mud-walled cell that it has filled with pollen and nectar. But it can't drill its own holes, so it nests in abandoned beetle holes in the old growth forests.

Needless to say, their native homes have dwindled, and so has their population. Armed with a drill bit, we can encourage these wonderful insects to build, live, and pollinate in our gardens. I learned about them when I was sent information on wholesale prices of orchard mason bees, since we are in the fruit tree business. I ordered a block of wood with 15 hibernating mason bees in it for $20. It came with another block of wood with 12 holes, each three inches deep, drilled with a 5/16 drill bit. (I can tell right away that these "hives" will be much easier to construct than honeybee hives.)

When the first flowers open in the spring, the warm weather has also awakened these small black bees. They knock out the mud wall and immediately mate, and then the work begins. The female gathers pollen and nectar and brings it back to the nesting hole. Then she lays an egg into this food provision and plugs the chamber with mud. She repeats this process again and again until the hole is filled with nesting chambers; then she plugs the opening with an extra-thick mud wall and looks for another hole. By having plenty of holes, we give her an opportunity to make plenty of babies.

By June, they're finished, and the adult bees die. Any crop that blooms after June, such as watermelons, will not benefit from orchard mason bees. It is the early blooming crops that these bees work with, especially fruit crops. Inside the nest, the egg hatches into a larva which eats the food, spins a cocoon, and turns into a pupa, which by the end of summer is a hibernating adult bee. You don't want to move the nests during this time, but by fall and winter, they can be shipped all across the country. These bees are gentle and not aggressive, although the female can sting if you squeeze her. Unlike honey bees, they don't have a hive to protect; all they are interested in is finding a hole and propagating.

Orchard mason bees only travel a few hundred yards from their nests for flowers and mud. The nests are hung where they get early morning sun, are protected from wind, and are near the orchard. Pesticides on the fruit trees will kill them and many other beneficial insects, along with the targeted pest. Look on the blooms of the first flowering shrubs in late February or early March. Flies have two wings and bees have four. Orchard mason bees are two-thirds the size of a honeybee and are shiny black.

I'd seen small black bees on our early blooming shrubs in the spring and wondered what they were. There are many kinds of small bees, but I'd never given them much thought. An orchardist, who doesn't keep bees, once told me his trees were pollinated by small black bees that are native to his area. By drilling holes in wooden blocks and hanging them in the orchard, we can increase the population of the orchard mason bee to help take up the slack the honeybee has left.

January 28, 1997

Insects

Bugs, bugs, bugs– there is no shortage of bugs. Biting, leaf chewing, worms, beetles, flies, you name it, we've got it. But of the many flying, crawling, hopping insects we have here, only a few are actually a nuisance. All bugs play an important role in our environment.

At night, you may see a big sphinx moth, a beautiful four inch wide flying creature with interesting and colorful markings. Soon you'll find their offspring, the tobacco or tomato hornworm, a big green worm, on your plants. Then along comes a parasitic wasp lying eggs on the back of the hornworm, and these white things sticking out of the worm suck it dry and dead. A few hornworms need to survive so that we get to see sphinx moths next year and so the wasps have something to feed on.

A fresh, green apple shoot is covered with aphids, or plant lice, one day. These small green bugs suck the juice out of the leaves, which curl up and wither. But along to the rescue come the ladybugs and lacewings that have been hiding out in a nearby vetch patch, to eat up the aphids.

All bugs have natural enemies. As we have moved cultivated plants from their original habitats, sometimes it takes a while for the balance to be restored. Mother Nature likes humus in her soils, or you could say the earth likes a rich black skin. Bugs are the supreme plant destroyers, turning green plants back into dead and decaying organic matter, and eventually into humus. Usually when bugs are attacking our crops, it's because our soils are not in the best condition.

How do bugs find the plants they feed on? A stressed out plant will send out signals that the bugs can pick up on. They will zoom in on weak plants to help Mother Nature create the ever-healing humus made by decaying plants. Beetles are more troublesome when the soil is compacted. An excess of nitrogen will invite aphids.

Beneficial insects, the ones that eat insect pests, can be encouraged to live in your garden by growing crops for them. Plants that attract them include crimson clover, Daikon radish, nasturtium, buckwheat and all the *Umbelliferae* family (parsley, dill, carrot, yarrow and caraway). Let a corner of your garden go wild with these plants and you'll have plenty of nectar and pollen for the good bugs, and a safe haven for them and other helpful beings.

I have burned beetles and spread the ash on the field, hoping to send a negative signal to the group soul of that specific pest. Blending them and spraying the crop with it will also say "this is not a good place for you."

Of course, I'm a bug predator, too, and feel no shame in squishing bean and potato beetles, squash bugs, and cabbage loopers. A spray of garlic juice helps repel bugs (unless they're Italian). The interplay of insects, the birds that eat them, the plants where beneficial bugs live, and the effect of each season's weather is so complicated that it can never be fully understood. It's a fascinating study and I'm convinced the insects bothering our crops are there to teach us something about farming.

So, I say bring on the bugs – the more the merrier. The flea beetles are eating the pigweed, and the praying mantis are devouring other insects, not to mention their own mates. Although frustrating at times, they are all working to improve the soil and the environment for future plant growth.

June 20, 1995

The Food Web

The food web is a recently coined term which replaces the more simplistic notion of a food chain. When I was in school, we learned about the food chain, which basically stated that the big fish eat the little fish, the little fish eat the smaller fish or plankton, and we eat the big fish. But it's much more complex than that, so now we'll try to understand our nourishment as an interactive web of connections, not a straight-line chain. My interest is in the soil food web and the role of microorganisms. Of course, my ultimate interest has been, and continues to be, "What's for dinner?" I no longer feel I'm at the top of a food chain, rather, I'm part of a food web, and my job is to feed the soil that feeds me and my customers, whose money keeps the farm afloat.

A leaf softly falls to the ground. A mouse may come by and nibble on it, a snake grabs the mouse, a hawk grabs the snake, the hawk gets bitten by the snake and dies, then the microbes eat the dead hawk. On the other hand, no mouse nibbles on the leaf, and the microbes eat it instead. The web is so complex, but eventually connects to the soil and the life in it. Watch the bees in the spring go from flower to flower. The nectar entices the bees in to coat their legs with pollen, which needs to be transferred to the next flower. Nature is fascinating, but the goal is simple - more life.

Why do plants sometimes have disease and insect problems? An unhealthy soil will have the desire to become more healthy (so nature can make more life), and dead plants help build soil. Beneficial and detrimental microbes reside in the soil. We classify them by the way they rot things. The ones that live with air help legumes fix nitrogen, suppress disease, produce amino acids and sugars, and then form antibiotics, vitamins, hormones and other substances which help plants grow healthily. The ones that live without air can also be beneficial when a useful fermentation takes place with photosynthetic bacteria. But often, an undesirable fermentation happens in airless places in the soil, and this is where the trouble starts. Ammonia, hydrogen sulfide and other harmful substances can be produced in an airless soil, which will smell bad. The soil will not correctly rot the crop residue because the wrong kinds of microbes are present. Specifically, it is fusarium fungi that causes so many disease problems. A large percentage of the world's crop land can be classified as disease-inducing soil, often because of the overpopulation of fusarium fungi.

Soil compaction (driving out the air) and too much nitrogen (without an appropriate amount of carbon to balance it) are the culprits. Proper tillage and adding organic matter are obvious measures to help the situation, and a combination of manures and cover crops will go a long way to restore the soils' microbial populations to a better balance. But there is new evidence that we can do more. After you've taken antibiotics for an illness, many doctors will recommend eating yogurt. This is because yogurt reintroduces beneficial microorganisms back into your freshly cleansed-out system where they can multiply and hold their own against undesirable intestinal flora. In the same way, we can introduce beneficial microorganisms back into fusarium-infested soils, and along with incorporating crop residues, manures and cover crops, transform the fields into disease-suppressing soils.

As scientists were studying this, they made a startling discovery. Individual microorganisms from various cultures, such as yeasts and yogurts, didn't really do the job, but where the scientists dumped their experiments, the soil life became greatly enhanced. It is the combination of many different microorganisms that can turn the soil around, just as manure or organic matter applied alone are not nearly as effective as when applied together. So, how do we get beneficial microorganisms? We grow them in the compost pile. With a billion in a tablespoon, a few yards of well-made compost can inoculate a large garden. The biodynamic preparations are teeming with these good guys, and teas made from rotting plants, particularly stinging nettle, are helpful too. Seaweed and other sea products also contain many of them.

Picture a rock, then a crack in the rock. Then a lichen growing in the crack in the rock. Then microbes living between the lichen and the rock. When an animal eats the lichen, the microbes eat the lichen's dead roots. The next lichen, or maybe moss this time, grows a little bigger than the first one. This is how soils are formed; by decaying plant roots. We can help dead roots decay by aerating the soil at the right time, because the soil microbial population, like any living being, needs air.

In summary, harmful microorganisms induce plant diseases, stimulate soil-born pathogens, immobilize plant nutrients, inhibit seed germination and hinder plant growth and development. Beneficial microorganisms help fix atmospheric nitrogen, decompose crop residue, suppress plant diseases and pathogens, recycle and make available plant nutrients, help form good soil structure, tie up heavy metals so plants don't take them up, and help to degrade toxic substances like pesticides. The food web is complex, but, luckily, we don't have to know all of the many connections. Our role is simply to feed the soil, bring it back to life and enjoy our daily bread.

April 29, 1997

Dandelion

Compositae Taxacum officanale

CHAPTER VII

Cow Horns and Crystals

The Agriculture Course	179
Homeopathy	186
Cow Horns	188
Horsetail Tea	191
Barrel Compost	193
Death and Life	195
Elementals	198
Planting by the Signs	200
Thanksgiving	203

"The proof of the pudding is in the eating."
Cervantes

The Agriculture Course

I. Vortex

By 1924 some European farmers had already noticed the deterioration of plant and animal health due to chemical fertilizers, and Rudolph Steiner responded by giving eight lectures in a course entitled "Agriculture", which this article attempts to summarize. He suggested we study the forces and processes at work in nature, not just the substances, and he stressed the need to fertilize our land with compost. With the proper numbers of animals, a healthy farm will produce all of its own food, feeds and fertilizers. The farm comes closest to its own essence when it can be conceived of as a kind of independent individuality, a self-contained entity. The soil is alive, it has an inherent plant-like vitality. A rich humus wants to become a plant. We do best to fertilize plants with humus which is plant life that has not reproduced but instead rotted or was eaten and excreted, i.e. compost and manure from our farm.

Just as a compass needle pointing north cannot be explained by the forces in the needle itself, plant growth has forces at work beyond the plant itself. The earth's magnetic field affects the needle, and forces beyond the earth affect the plant. A seed has two distinct futures - it can fall to the ground to grow or become humus, or it can be eaten by a member of a higher kingdom of nature. A plant lives between two polarities: calcium - or earthly - forces, which promote growth and flowering, and silica - or cosmic - forces, which support ripening and nutrition. Earth and water energy help the plant to grow and reproduce, pushing from below, while air and warmth pull the plant from above and help the food ripen and become more nutritious.

Picture the concentric circles of the planets revolving around the sun, and then remember that the sun is actually whizzing through space with the planets trailing behind it, creating a huge vortex. The earth is in the middle of this vortex. Mars, Jupiter and Saturn are on the outside, the moon, Venus and Mercury are on the inside, and each side has opposite affects. The soil's silica content absorbs forces from Mars, Jupiter and Saturn and radiates them back upward; calcium works with forces from the moon, Venus and Mercury which radiate downward.

These forces have to work with the substances, the elements, of the earth. What we understand about these substances through chemistry is superficial, like the knowledge we can get from a photograph of a person. We need to get to know them in their essence, their deeper nature and their relationships.

II. Chemistry

Sulfur is the carrier of the spirit. It's name is related to phosphorus, and both are known as the light-bearers. They are anions (negative ions).

Carbon is the carrier of all of nature's formative processes. The spirit activity of the universe works as a sculptor, moistening its fingers with sulfur and, with carbon's help, build up the form an anything that's alive. Animals and people are mobile because our breathing expels carbon, whereas the rooted plant world absorbs carbon dioxide from the air and retains it. All living things have an underlying framework of carbon, with lime-like substances as the earthly formative forces, and silica-like substances as the cosmic formative forces. If we look at the world as the physical manifestation of the spirit, we realize that the spirit needs a physical carrier. Carbon is this carrier of form for the spirit.

For life, the carrier is oxygen, again with sulfur's help. Form moves along the paths of carbon, and life moves along the paths provided by oxygen. Oxygen is related to the water element; carbon is related to the earth element.

Nitrogen is the mediator between life (oxygen) and spirit, which temporarily assumes form in carbon. Nitrogen is the great transporter, carrying oxygen into the carbon. But nitrogen has something else - with the help of sulfur, nitrogen carries sensitivity. When we meditate, we hold back some of the carbon dioxide in our breath, we become a little stiffer, so to speak, and we experience the nitrogen, what the nitrogen "senses," and what it can teach us. The nitrogen is related to the air element and senses what is going on, for example, on the farm. The farmer, walking through the field, picks up on whatever nitrogen is sensing, and, regulated by love and enthusiasm, intuitively knows what's best for the land. Just as our soul mediates between our worldly life and the spirit, nitrogen (sensitivity) helps the oxygen (life) find the carbon (spirit).

Everything that lives on earth and assumes a physical form must be led back to the spirit. Hydrogen, again with the help of sulfur, has this responsibility. It relates to the fire element and dissolves and disperses everything. These elements - sulfur, carbon, oxygen, nitrogen and hydrogen - are spiritual processes or forces with specific roles in the realm of nature.

Lime has a remarkable relationship to the world of human desires. As calcium, it has all kinds of cravings and wants to combine with oxygen and other elements. Lime pulls at us. Something like desire is always present in lime. It is soft, soluble, and found on the insides of animals and plants, like in our bones or in the seed of an apple. Other lime-like elements are the other cations (positive ions) - magnesium, potassium and sodium. On the other hand, silica is always found on the periphery; for instance, in your hair and fingernails and the peel of the apple. It is non-soluble, hard and self-content. Something like perception is present in silica crystals. In earthly existence, silica is generalized outer perception, lime is generalized outer desire, and mediating in between them is clay. Our soils need the forces of lime, clay and sand.

Dr. Steiner sure makes a chemistry class interesting, doesn't he? He says our task is to understand the earth organism as a whole, then we can also see the role each plant species plays. The legumes, for example, with their flowers and fruits close to the ground and their ability to fix atmospheric nitrogen, are the in-breathing organs of the earth. Other plants have other functions.

III. Horn Manure and Horn Silica

An important question is: "How do we bring nitrogen into our soils to fertilize our crops?" Most of what we eat is not absorbed into the body as substance; it is excreted. It is there in order to convey forces to the body. Our concern is not the correct amounts of food, but the vitality of the forces in the food. Fertilizing must consist of providing the soil with vitality. Plants want to grow in something living: humus-like substances in the process of decomposition. There is an intimate relationship between the plant and the surrounding soil, with no sharp dividing line between them. The most important thing is that when the food reaches the human being, its effect on human life should be as beneficial and health-giving as possible. We can't do this using artificial fertilizers because they influence only the water element, not the earthly element.

In compost, we have a means for enlivening the earthly element. Rotting substances have the nitrogen forces in the necessary form to give back to the earth, so that we can bring our food to the proper energetic state. Dr. Steiner gave the indications for what are now known as the biodynamic field sprays and compost preparations by first asking, "Why does a cow have horns and a stag have antlers?" The cow, a calm, content animal with four stomachs, has horns to radiate nitrogen and oxygen forces back into its digestive system. Their manure is the best plant food and is full of these forces. The stag's antlers, on the other hand, direct its forces outward. It is a nervous animal with an intense communication with its surrounding environment.

We stuff manure into a cow horn and bury it in the earth in the fall and through the winter. In the spring, we dig it up and, amazingly, the manure has turned into a humus-like substance. The next step is to take a quarter-cup of the horn manure and stir it in a bucket with three gallons of water. First, we make a vortex by rapidly stirring the mixture for twenty seconds in one direction and then reverse directions to create a bubbling chaos and a vortex in the other direction. We continue alternating directions for one whole hour. This is then sprinkled on an acre of plowed land. The horn manure works with the calcium or earthly forces - growth and reproductivity - and is stirred and sprayed in the evening.

To help balance this, we grind quartz crystals into a powder, mix with enough water to make a paste and again put it in a cow horn, but this time we bury it during the spring and summer. Half a teaspoon of the horn silica is similarly stirred homeopathically with three gallons of water for an hour, but early in the morning. It works with the silica or cosmic forces - ripening and nutrition - and is sprayed as the sun is rising.

Chapter 7 Cow Horns and Crystals

Even as late as the mid-19th century, instinctual peasant wisdom was still present. We've lost that now, but, along with retaining our present intellectual understandings, we need to regain it. People back then knew that through certain practices they could make themselves fit for tending plants. Delicate and subtle influences are lost if you are among people who don't heed such things.

Fertilizing with the horn manure and horn silica is not meant to replace manuring in the usual way. We must continue good farming practices. The soil around the plant roots is a living entity with a vegetative life of its own. When we send products off of the farm, we are taking forces away from the soil which need to be replenished. We need to infuse the manure and compost with living forces, which are more valuable to the plant than the mere substances. Radiant forces are released when small quantities are applied in the right way.

IV. The Compost Preparations

The six biodynamic compost preparations are plants treated in a special way, then placed in compost or manure piles in very small amounts. A teaspoon is sufficient for a 10 ton pile. They radiate the forces of the elements and help them come together in the right way so that the interaction of the plants and the soil creates truly healthy food, for both animals and people.

Yarrow is a miracle of creation because of the ideal way it brings sulfur into relationship with other substances. Its mere presence in the fields is beneficial. The flowers are picked and enclosed in a stag's bladder, hung up in the sunshine during the summer, and then buried during winter months. What is present in yarrow is strongly preserved in the bodies of humans and animals in the process that takes place between the kidneys and bladder. Yarrow is used medicinally for bladder and kidney ailments. By putting the yarrow in the stag's bladder, the inherent sensitivity of the deer enhances the yarrow's ability to combine sulfur with other substances.

Chamomile is a wonderful plant that works with calcium. It is stuffed into a cow's intestine, and these sausages are buried in the ground for a year. It helps stabilize the nitrogen in the compost. Stinging nettle works with iron radiations, and the role it plays in nature is similar to the heart. It is buried, surrounded by peat moss, for a whole year and a half. Its use will make the soil more intelligent. Oak bark has a unique quality of calcium in it that, when specially prepared, counteracts diseases on the farm. It is chopped up and put into the skull of a cow or sheep and buried under running water, such as a small brook or stream.

Dandelion is another beneficial plant on our farms, a messenger from heaven mediating the relationship between silica and potassium in the soil. The flowers are packed into a cow's stomach lining, the mesentery, and buried through the winter. Valerian flowers are simply pressed, the juice stirred homeopathically with water, and then sprinkled on the compost pile to help stimulate the workings of phosphorus. These preparations enliven the compost and the soil to such a degree that nitrogen can be brought into the soil by the transmutation of elements. Under the influence of hydrogen, lime and potassium are transmuted into a distinctly beneficial nitrogen.

V. Ashes and Horsetail

Dr. Steiner also gave us indications for experiments to counteract problems on the farm with weeds, animals, insects and diseases. All living things can only live within a certain range of conditions and forces. Agriculture is the art of creating conditions and working with forces. Forces are concentrated in the seed. To combat weed problems, we burn weed seeds, homeopathically potentize the ash, and sprinkle it on the land. After doing this for four consecutive years, these weeds will be weakened because the moon's growth effects are canceled. It worked for the thistles in our pasture.

For a rodent infestation, we burn the skin of a mouse when Venus is in the constellation Scorpio. The ash contains the negative of the mouse's reproductive force, and again is homeopathically prepared and spread around the farm or barnyard. The constellations from Aquarius through Cancer have to do with the insect world, so for an insect problem, we gather the whole bugs and burn them when the sun is in Taurus. This ash spreads destructive forces to the bugs in question when applied on the farm.

Too much moon force creates plant parasites or diseases. Tea from the silica-rich horsetail plant is homeopathically prepared and helps dry up the plants, strengthening the air and light forces.

In nature, and throughout the universe, everything is in mutual interaction with everything else. Certain species of birds and insects perform specific functions in nature, and we have no way of comprehending all of these interactions. Birds regulate the nitrogen forces around trees and forests, while insects regulate nitrogen forces around herbaceous plants in the meadows and fields. Earthworms regulate the oxygen forces of life in the soil. Conifers are important for the birds, shrubs are important for the mammals, and damp areas are needed for frogs and mushrooms. All of these are vitally important for farming, so we need to preserve the woods, hedgerows and wetlands on our farms because of the forces they contain.

Biodynamic preparations can help plants become more sensitive. They are able to absorb what they need from the surrounding fields, forests and meadows. As I pondered this idea one day in the corn patch, I thought to myself, "Where is this corn going to get phosphorus and nitrogen from if I don't put it there?" Just then, a bird from the nearby woods flew by and the gift it dropped fed my faith, along with feeding the corn.

Dr. Steiner was asked once, "Why do people show so little evidence of spiritual experience? Why is the will for carrying out spiritual impulses so weak? How can we carry out spiritual intentions without being pulled off the path by personal ambition, illusions and petty jealousy?" His surprising answer was, "This is a problem of nutrition. Nutrition as it is today does not supply the strength necessary for manifesting the spirit in physical life. A bridge can no longer be built from thinking to will and action. Food plants no longer contain the forces people need for this." Steiner's Agriculture Course, available as a book entitled <u>Agriculture</u>, was an attempt to give farmers ideas and impulses to correct this situation.

July 30, 1996

Homeopathy

Horn manure is a homeopathic preparation full of enzymatic activity that supports the growth and reproductive processes in plants and helps the soil to build humus. A quarter-cup of it is stirred for one hour in three gallons of water then sprinkled on an acre of land. To better understand how such a small quantity could have an effect, we can look at homeopathy, whose founder, Samuel Haueneman, lived a few hundred years ago. He was a doctor who gradually discovered a way to use very small, potentized doses of medicines to cure his patients.

Homeopathy bases its cures on all of the symptoms a patient has. A homeopathic doctor not only wants to know where you hurt, but about how you sleep, what foods taste good or bad, how your memory is working and many other seemingly unrelated questions. But of course they are all related, as the totality of anyone's experiences make up the person. Homeopathy recognizes two other bodies besides the physical one - an emotional body and a mental body. Any disorder in the physical body has a counter disorder in the emotional and mental bodies. They are all related.

Through extensive experiments on himself and his colleagues, Haueneman discovered that all medicine affected not only his physical body, but his emotional and mental bodies as well. They would take medicines for days or weeks at a time and record all they felt emotionally; such as happiness, depression, anxiety, aloofness; mentally, such as thinking clearly, forgetfulness, day dreaming, illogical thoughts; and physical symptoms, such as soreness, muscle cramps, achy bones. The results were gathered in a huge work we now know as the Materia Medica. Each plant and mineral medicine has certain effects on each of the three bodies.

Haueneman rediscovered the ancient adage "like cures like." For instance, when the cure for malaria - quinine - is taken by a healthy person, it produces the same symptoms malaria does. The remedy is chosen by looking at a list of the patient's symptoms in all three categories - physical, emotional and mental - and comparing them to the list of observations from the Materia Medica. The one closest to the patient's symptoms is the cure. For example, a dose of poison ivy is the cure for a poison ivy rash, but the dose has to be very small and potentized. The other principal of homeopathy is that the healing qualities of a medicine are greatly enhanced by the process known as potentizing, which involves shaking one part of the medicine in nine parts water for three minutes to get what is called D1. One part of D1 is then shaken with nine parts of water for another three minutes to produce D2. It only has one-hundredth of the original medicine in it, and D3 only one-thousandth. By the time you get up to D30 (minus 10 to the 30th power), there is not even one molecule of the original medicine left, but the remedy is now extremely effective.

It seemed pretty far-fetched to me, to say the least, and I was quite surprised to learn that at the turn of the century, one out of every six doctors in New York City, and one out of every eight nationwide, was a homeopathic doctor. The amazing thing is that, if you get the right remedy, it works. We have a small kit with 40 or so different remedies to choose from, some for colds or flu, some for nervous disorders or stomach problems, some for when you start to get sick and others for after you're already ill. Each remedy is a very small amount of the actual medicine, maybe one billionth or so. But by the process of potentizing, the healing capacities are brought out to stimulate all three bodies - not just the physical - to heal themselves by waking up the natural immune system. Many doctors use homeopathy today as a very safe and effective medical practice, and biodynamic practitioners are using it to help improve farmland.

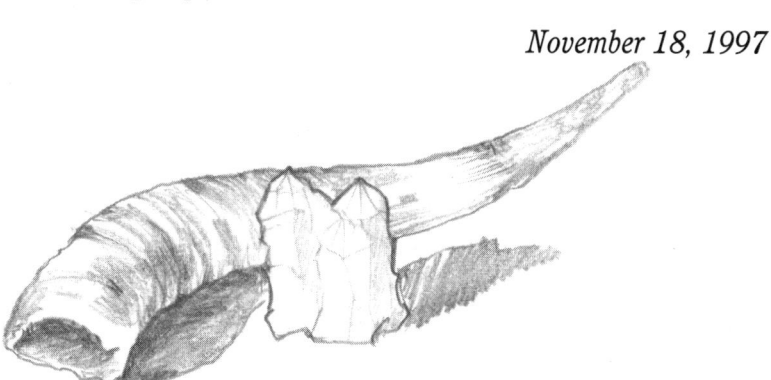

November 18, 1997

Cow Horns

In Dr. Steiner's Agriculture course, he spoke out against the use of artificial fertilizers and promoted compost instead. He also gave us the recipes for horn manure and horn silica. Cow horns are vortexial-shaped appendages on the cow's head that send back forces the cow does not use in its nervous system. The cow is a digestive animal, the supreme grass digester. She turns out the supreme plant food, manure. Since the cow does not fully use its head and nervous system, Steiner said oxygen and nitrogen forces were sent back to the manure via the horns.

So we take this wonderful manure and bury it in cow horns over the winter in good garden soil when the earth is most alive. Why is the earth more alive in winter than in summer? Think about all the potential growth, invisible until summer, stored underground during winter in roots and seeds. Crystallizing forces are strong then, too, as the snow and ice remind us. During this burial process, an actual homeopathic potentizing of the manure takes place, and the change it undergoes is undeniable. It turns into a rich, black substance. I have buried cow manure in a goat horn and in a glass jar right next to the cow horns, and when I dug them up, the manure in them was still green and stinky. Only in the cow horns did it change into a humus-like substance, and scientific analysis reveals it to be teeming with enzymes.

What are enzymes? Enzymes are biocatalysts of the processes that build up amino acids in proteins. Although small and invisible, they are mighty workers in the bodies of plants and animals. Raw foods are good for you because they contain enzymes. Enzymes are in the soil, too, and their presence insures that certain life processes can occur.

The ratio is a quarter cup to three gallons per acre, so to treat eight acres I take two cups of horn manure and put it into a 50 gallon crock half full of slightly warmed, clear spring water. Because of the negative effects that trace amounts of chemicals may have on these forces, only clean buckets and crocks are used. Now I stir it up, and this is done with great enthusiasm. I stir at the edge of the crock and develop a deep uniform vortex all the way to the bottom. A vortex is a wonderful thing, a common form in plant growth, running water, the movement of galaxies and atoms, and weather phenomena. Once I get a deep whirlpool going, I switch hands and begin stirring in the other direction. Now, instead of this nice orderly vortex, I have chaos, with the seething and foaming water trying to continue one way while I'm trying to make it go the other way.

Of course my human will wins out, and the vortex is soon spinning nice and neatly in the other direction. Then I switch hands again and reverse it, creating another chaos. I stir clockwise with my left hand and counter clockwise with my right. I repeat this vortex, chaos, vortex, chaos potentizing process for one hour. Now the potentized manure has potentized the water, so the next step is to potentize the falling dew. Did you ever think about how the earth breathes every day? As the dew settles at night, the earth is breathing in.

I dip the stirred horn manure water out of the crock and strain it through an old T-shirt into the spray rig behind my tractor. I stir late in the day so I can spray the land right after I finish stirring, just at dusk when you can feel moisture in the air. The potentized dew then carries the forces of the horn manure into the soil. I try to get it on 10 acres of pasture at least once a year, with the garden getting it two or three times.

In the morning, as the fog lifts with the sun, the earth is breathing out, and this is when we stir and spray horn silica, which balances the horn manure. Instead of a dark humus made from manure, horn silica is white and made from beautiful quartz crystal, and instead of spending the winter months underground it is buried in the spring.

Rainbow sparkling crystals, either from local geodes or Arkansas mines, are hammered on an anvil into small chunks and dropped into an inverted steel fence post driver. A tamper bar and a good bit of zeal further crush the crystals, and then they are poured thru a strainer. A spoonful at a time is rubbed between two windowpanes until it is ground to the consistency of cornmeal. Water is added to make a paste and then it gets packed into the cow horns and buried about a foot deep. After it is dug up in the late fall we empty it into a glass jar and store it on a sunny windowsill. The stirring procedure is the same as for the horn manure but you only need a half teaspoon per acre with the three gallons of water and it is done at the crack of dawn.

When I first learned about this, I thought, "This is the most foolish hogwash I've ever heard," but I kept discovering that it was done on wonderfully fertile farms. I thought, "Well, if a farmer pays that much attention to details, they are bound to be good farmers, and it's not the preparation at all." Faith may be sufficient to move mountains, but it is not necessary. The mountains move on their own. I was encouraged to try this weird ordeal, on the premise that it would work even if I did not believe it. Being the experimental skeptic that I am, and deep into learning about how to build soil humus, I accepted the challenge and have been stirring ever since. I started by stirring in a five-gallon plastic bucket and sprinkling an acre with a whisk broom, feeling like a (somewhat embarrassed) priest in some ancient ritual. I hoped my neighbors didn't see me and ask me to explain.

But seemingly magical transformations started happening in our soils. Yellow land turned brown, and brown soils turned black, much more than the amount of compost, manure or cover crops could account for. And, as I suspected, I became more attuned to details and observations as to what the farm was doing as a whole. It has taken me 10 years to finally make a real good quality horn manure preparation, and I'm still learning how to stir and spray it properly. Very few people have taken up this work, and there is a huge amount to learn.

It was last fall when I got a real insight into the value of this procedure, oddly enough from a soil scientist who sincerely believes in chemical agriculture. He was impressed with the fertility in our garden and cropland, which he attributed to compost, manure and cover crops. Even the most ardent chemical agriculture teacher still believes these are good ideas. But what struck home were his comments about our pasture soils.

"This is unlike 95% of the land I've seen in Tennessee," he said. The softness experienced while walking on it spoke of organic matter and life, and the color implied fertility. This land had received very little, if any, compost – only the manure from the cows that lived there and the horn manure preparation. It wasn't until later, when we walked on the new land I'd just bought, that he said, "Now, this is more typical of Tennessee soils, hard and lighter in color." I hope he can come back in a few years after we've been applying the cow horn preparations.

November 25, 1997

Chapter 7 Cow Horns and Crystals

Horsetail Tea

The purpose of fungi in the household of nature is to decay plant material so that it turns into life-giving humus. I love to see old dead plants rotting quickly, covered with molds and mushrooms. But when a live plant starts to mold, something is unhealthy. Often there is a nutrient deficiency or an unbalanced soil, making the plant weak, so the fungi appear to do their job.

You could say a plant doesn't really get a disease - there is just too much life energy around it. Because the plant can't grow fast enough, a parasite can appear. Usually this excess energy is in the form of water, and the parasite is said to be a disease. Rich compost and a humus soil will absorb a lot of fungal activity, keeping it down in the soil. Some of our older garden beds sprout mushrooms, and I feel this is a healthy sign. Fungi belong in the soil, not on the plants.

Water is connected to the moon, so you could say a "diseased" plant has too much moon energy. If the weather is too dry, you can water your garden, but what do you do if it's too wet? Inside a double-pane window, you may find a bag of dessicant. It absorbs moisture so the windows don't fog up. Dessicant is also used in storage jars to keep stuff dry. It is made of ground silica. Silica is very common, making up about half of the earth's crust. It is a combination of the elements silicon and oxygen. Sand is silica. So are quartz crystals. Silica is found on the skin and peels of fruits and vegetables. Because it is so hard and slick, water runs off it. An apple would never store well if its peel was as soft as its insides.

A sandy soil dries out much faster after a rain than a clay soil. Adding sand to our clay soils will benefit them, especially in a wet season. Sulfur is a traditional and effective spray for fungus problems, but it is rather harsh on beneficial insects and other life forms because it is so acidic. How about a silica spray? In nature, there is one plant with much more silica in it than any other. Horsetail, *equisetum arvenses*, has a silica content of 90% of its dry matter. Horsetail is an unusual plant, growing along waterways and swampy places. The plant is all stalk and no leaf, and the hollow sections of the stalk pop apart at their nodes.

I simmer a pint of the dried plant in a few gallons of water for an hour or so. Then I strain it into a five-gallon bucket, put a lid on it, and let it ferment for a few weeks. It develops a lemony smell after a while. Many people use the tea directly, without fermenting it, especially in greenhouse production where the lack of air flow exacerbates fungal problems. Before I spray the horsetail tea, I stir one part of it with nine parts water, alternating direction about every 20 seconds. The building of a vortex and the resulting chaos when you change directions creates a homeopathic potentizing effect. After 20 minutes, I pour it into my backpack sprayer and set the nozzle to a fine mist. I like to spray horsetail tea early in the morning, when no wind is blowing and no rain is forecast. It is the soft-leaved plants that particularly need this help: tomatoes, potatoes, squash and beans. Silica counters the earth and water forces of humus with light and warmth forces.

The use of horsetail tea, like a garlic spray and other organic practices, is a preventive measure. It's a plant protector, not a fungus killer. The specific disease names interest me less now than the conditions which encourage them and how we can discourage these underlying conditions. The ability of molds, fungi and "diseases" to quickly decay and transform unhealthy plants helps clean up the household of nature and prepares the way for new growth. Nature supplies us with silica to help check these forces when they run rampant from excess moisture during rainy spells. Maybe a chant would help too, something like, "rain, rain, go away, come again some other day."

November 18, 1997

Chapter 7 Cow Horns and Crystals

Barrel Compost

Barrel compost is a specially prepared, biodynamic compound used to help decompose organic matter and build soil humus. I made a couple of batches years ago, and finally got around to doing it again. Steve and Furrow donated an old wooden barrel they weren't using, and I was in business.

The German scientist, Maria Thun, came up with the recipe for barrel compost after studying various forms of calcium and their effect on plants and atomic radiation. In 1958, after the atom bomb tests, the strontium 90 levels in plants were highest when they were grown on granite soils and less prevalent where the plants were grown on limestone soils. Her research was done with oats, celery and tomatoes, as those plants tend to collect strontium 90, a harmful radioactive substance released in nuclear fission. Eggshells and basalt rock powder were found to be helpful. Basalt is a volcanic rock with all the elements in it which become clay, sort of an infant clay. We don't have basalt here in Tennessee, but there are mountains of it out West and in New England, which is where I got a couple of pounds. Basalt can be spread directly on a garden to help the humus formation in clay soils.

The finished barrel compost is stirred in water, alternating directions a couple of times a minute for 20 minutes, then sprayed on the soil in the evening to help the soil digest cover crops and turn the manure, green manure and soil into a wonderful humus. After the nuclear accident at Chernobyl, aerial photographs showed a few spots of land that were not emitting radioactivity. These turned out to be farms which had used barrel compost. This unfortunate tragedy validated Maria Thun's research.

The egg shape of the wooden barrel is nice, as it has no sharp angles, but barrel compost can be made in a brick-lined pit if no barrel is available. The whiskey odor from an old Jack Daniels barrel can be removed by serious scrubbing with lye soap and rinsing with a stinging nettle tea. Steve's barrel had been a doghouse, and it had been many years since its life as a whiskey barrel, so I just hosed it down and started looking for a good spot to dig a hole. We came upon a place under well-grown trees in a hedgerow near the garden, and soon had a major excavation going. I set the barrel in the two foot deep hole, open side down, and then filled in around it with good soil, sloping up to the top of the rim. An axe easily took out the top wooden slats, and I threw a bucket of finished compost into the buried, open-ended cylinder.

Back in the pasture I had gathered five buckets (25 gallons) of fresh cow manure, having looked especially for those nice folded cowpies, but settling for some pretty loose ones, too. I dumped this onto a piece of plywood and added 1,100 grams of basalt rock and 200 grams of ground eggshells. Then I mixed it all up with a shovel for a full hour. A piece of 1/2 inch mesh hardware cloth, nailed to an empty window frame, covered the top of the barrel, and we squished our mixture through it. This helps aerate it and further potentizes it, but it was quite time consuming.

After filling the barrel halfway, we inserted a teaspoon each of the biodynamic preparations into it, with yarrow in the north, valerian in the south, dandelion in the west, chamomile in the east, and stinging nettle and oak bark in the center. I also put horn manure in the very center, in between the last two. We set the screen back on top and continued pressing the manure mixture through it as darkness fell. We finished by candlelight, adding another set of the preparations in the same positions, and then covered the barrel with a large, flat slate rock.

I'll remix it again after six weeks and add more of the herbal preparations. When it has turned into a rich, dark humus substance, I'll consider it done and use it at the rate of 1/2 cup to three gallons of water per acre. I know from experience that it will build up our soil's humus, but I hope we don't have to find out the hard way about its role in mitigating the effects of radiation. Any kind of soil humus helps buffer against negative environmental concerns, but barrel compost, with its brand new calcium via the chamomile, oak bark, eggshells and basalt, amplifies this protection. It's chock full of enzymes, and you might say it makes your garden a more comfortable place for elemental beings, or nature spirits. I'll have extra if anyone would like to try it.

April 11, 2000

Chapter 7 Cow Horns and Crystals

Death and Life

Old hay can kill a cow, as I found out the hard way. I had cleaned some bright yellow hay out of an old barn, and instead of following my first inclination to throw it on the asparagus patch, decided on second thought to toss it on some poor pasture land. Two jersey milk cows ate it and bloated. Debby came up on the horrible sight of a dead cow and our favorite milker, Annie, near death. She quickly got help, and through the loving dedication and speed of our veterinarian, they jabbed a hole in the cow to let out the gas. I am happy to report Annie is doing well, though we fear she may have lost her calf.

Marcie, on the other hand, was history. But I realized she still had something to offer to the farm. In biodynamics, the farming method which puts emphasis on the forces in nature rather than the substances, we use animal organs to wrap herbs with to make homeopathic remedies for use in the compost piles. Although I've made the preparations before, I had never used organs from my own cows. The time had come. Chris and Christy are organic farmers living in Kentucky who study Rudolf Steiner's 1924 lecture course on agriculture and try to implement it on their farm. Fortunately, Chris has a stronger stomach than I and was able to come help.

I spent the morning sowing the wheat and harrowing it into the field, needing the grounding that such a job offers. Chris punctured the dead bloated cow, which sounded like a tire going flat and smelled like a closed roomful of football players eating beans and cabbage. When he started severing the head, I offered to take his two daughters to get oak bark. "To have a healing effect, the calcium (that we must bring into our manure) must remain within the realm of life ... ordinary lime is of no use," said Steiner, as he points to white oak bark, which contains 77% calcium. To concentrate its healing forces, we must stuff the bark into the skull of a domestic animal and bury it under a stream of water over the winter.

When I got back with the bark, collected from the largest white oak on our farm, Debby and Christy were helping Chris figure out what exactly the mesentery was. We needed this to wrap up the dandelion flowers which I had picked several springs ago and had dried and stored for this occasion. We got a few slabs of Marcie's innards and a section of her small intestines. Debby and Christy both had dried chamomile flowers to donate for an odd sort of sausage making. Back by the creek, Christy rinsed the intestines out, Chris carved excess meat off the head, and I (conveniently) went into the kitchen to light a fire and make tea. I picked dandelion leaves for the tea to rehydrate the dried dandelion flowers and made chamomile tea to moisten the chamomile flowers. I found an old hand grinder in the barn and ground up the oak's inner bark, which was not what flakes off the tree first, but the reddish-colored bark that I pried off with the claw of a hammer.

Debby and Christy stuffed the moist chamomile flowers into foot long sections of the cow's intestines. Chamomile flowers make a soothing and relaxing tea that is good for stomach aches. They also have sulfur and calcium in just the right proportion and quality to make a preparation which gives manure the power to receive enough life into itself so that it can transmit it back to the soil. Chris put the bloody skull in the truck bed, as it was time to go to a water faucet to hose out the brains. At this point, we realized the mesentery we had was a stomach, so we needed to go back to the cow. I grabbed a copy of Gray's Anatomy, and Chris looked up mesentery while we drove up the hill.

In his lecture, Steiner says by mesentery he means the peritoneum, but I think these are different. We found a thin membrane surrounding the intestines and decided that was what we needed. We sewed the dandelion flowers, the first and last blooming plants on our farm, into the peritoneum or mesentery, still not quite sure which we had. This preparation allows the plant to become inwardly sensitive and able to draw to itself all that it needs. We then used a wire to stir up the brains and a spoon to remove them from the skull, and flushed it out with a hose. After stirring, scooping and flushing several times, we were ready to refill it. I dampened the ground-up and sifted oak bark, and we packed it tightly into the skull. Here a high-calcium plant material from a highly evolved plant, the white oak, is being surrounded by a high-calcium animal part, the brain cavity, of a highly evolved animal, the cow. This preparation will strengthen the forces which combat plant diseases.

Chapter 7 Cow Horns and Crystals

By now we were working by the light of our 12-volt porch light, and it was "big dark" out. We put everything in buckets out of dog's reach and went into the house to eat a baked potato. I can hardly believe we had much of an appetite, but the 'taters disappeared one by one. Chris, bless his soul, loved my comment, "Well, you're the only friends I would invite to do this with." Christy showed her appreciation , "You sure know how to throw a party, Jeff." I certainly would not have tackled this job without them.

The next morning, I dug a hole and set the tight chamomile sausages (wrapped in some hardware cloth to keep out animals) about a foot deep, packed soil around them, and filled the hole back up. In a different spot, I did the same with the dandelion preparation. I covered the hole in the skull with an old piece of bone and buried it in the stream behind the barn, then put some wire and big rocks over it to keep dogs from getting it. In June, I sewed up yarrow flowers in a stag's bladder which is hung in the sun for the summer and also spends the winter underground. Stinging nettle is buried in a screen pillow (to keep earthworms out) surrounded by peat moss for over a year. Valerian flowers get squeezed and the juices fermented, which are diluted with water and stirred before the mixture is added to the compost piles.

In the spring, around Pentecost, I will dig up the preparations and store them in the root cellar. A teaspoon of each one will be inserted into the 10-ton compost piles I'll make from hay, manure and soil where I feed the cattle over the winter. The soil treated with these remarkable preparations, full of enzymes and life-giving properties, allows the plants to fully interact with the forces of nature.

At the very least, it seems like the making of the preparations would enhance the powers of observation and caring of the farmer and facilitate the interconnectedness of the farm. After the humbling experience of stupidly letting my cows eat old hay, I certainly feel the need to be more observant, careful and interconnected.

November 17, 1998

Elementals

Both Greek philosophers and Oriental sages have regarded earth, water, air and fire as the four elements which make up the world. Indeed, as we observe nature, everything falls into one of these categories - solid, liquid, gaseous and heat. Back when people weren't so "smart" (intellectual), they perceived beings at work in these elements.

Gnomes are one of the names given to the invisible earth creatures that know all about minerals and ores. I can imagine them working underground, bringing to the plant roots the calcium, potassium, and phosphorous, along with the trace elements - boron, copper, iron, magnesium, sulfur, cobalt, manganese, zinc and molybdenum - which the plant needs in order to grow. The earthworms must be their helpers, and the gnomes use the fallen forms of decaying plants as images during the winter to build up new plants for next spring. I've been looking for morel mushrooms recently, and a "dryland fish" somehow reminds me of these dwarves, with their seemingly magical appearances and funny hats. Toads also have a gnome-like vibe.

The water beings are active in the chemistry of combining substances together to create the plant's leaves. The leaf's veins, spreading out in the foliage, are their work in bringing the minerals into the realm of life. Fish are the animals associated with the water beings.

Working in the air to bring light to the plants are the elves, who enjoy the flight of birds. The margins of leaves, which so differentiate the plant world, are their gesture. As the plant grows toward flowering, these light and air beings refine the leaves into the calyx which will then burst forth into blossom.

The fire beings bring warmth to the flowers and carry the pollen from anther to pistil, where fertilization occurs to bring forth the new seed. Their activity is made visible in the interaction of insects, particularly butterflies and blossoms.

As ancient cultures looked out at the world, they perceived the workings of these elemental beings building up the plants. Modern-day initiates, like Rudolf Steiner, also describe these beings. The magic of the Findhorn gardens in Scotland is attributed to communication with the "devas," and I've read about other people talking with elemental beings or nature spirits.

Sorry, folks, but I don't. I do know that I know very little of what goes on and oftentimes work from intuition, but always with some rationalization. I may spread compost to help the earth beings, but I think, "the plant roots need the elements in the compost." I may plant flowers to make the air and fire beings happy, but I know the birds and insects that love sunflowers are beneficial to the garden. How do we know where an act of will originates? Some people talk to their plants, believing the plants respond to their chatter. That could be, but I feel odd talking to animals, let alone plants. Maybe a silent communication takes place, but it's deep in my subconsciousness.

A good farmer will move cattle one day, sow seed another day, and may not be able to explain why. I consider this an intuitive grasp of the whole farm organism, resulting from years and generations of farming decisions based on a time when our livelihood and meals were a direct consequence of our daily activities. I don't doubt some people see and talk to nature spirits, but some of them may be locked up in institutions, as their other faculties are lacking in proportion to the prospering of these imaginations.

Take a four-foot section of one-inch pipe and look through it. Sometimes that is how much of reality I feel I actually perceive. If I took the pipe away and saw it all, I'd probably go crazy, so I'll just keep looking through my narrow band of reality. But that doesn't stop me from imagining what else might be out there.

April 4, 2000

Planting by the Signs

Planting by the signs is an ancient practice still widely used today. The signs are the twelve constellations of stars that lie in the same plane as our solar system, making a huge circle around it. In the winter, the sun rises in the southeast and at noon is about 30 degrees above the southern horizon in our latitude of 36 degrees, and then sets in the southwestern sky. In the summer, it rises in the northeast and at noon is 72 degrees above the southern horizon, setting in the northwest. This strip of sky is where you will always find the sun, the moon, and the visible planets. It is divided into twelve sections, each one defined by a group of stars. These are the constellations of the Zodiac, better known as the signs. Farmer's almanacs describe the attributes and folklore of the signs and provide a calendar.

For example, on July 15, 1997, the sun was in front of the sign Gemini, and the moon was in front of the sign Libra, but moved into Scorpio later in the day. Venus was in front of Leo, and you could see them both in the western sky at sunset. The backward question mark is the head of Leo, and the right triangle behind it are the legs. With a little imagination, you can see the lion. The brightest star is the planet Venus. It takes about a month for the sun to move from one sign to the next, a year to complete all twelve. The moon changes signs every few days and passes through all twelve in about a month. When people talk about planting by the signs, they are referring to the moon's position in front of particular constellations, and whether it's waxing or waning.

Libra and Aries are small groups of stars and the moon is only in them for a little over two days. Virgo and Gemini are big constellations that each house the moon for four days. Each of the signs represents an animal or picture and a particular part of the human body. They are also related to the four elements and the different parts of plants. The chart summarizes those relationships.

When the moon is in front of one of the fire signs, Ram, Lion or Archer, then you plant and work with crops that bear fruit or seeds, such as corn, beans and melons. Root crops, like carrots, beets and potatoes, are planted when the moon is in an earth sign, the Bull, Virgin or Goat. Flowers are planted in an air sign, and greens or hay

Constellation	Sign	Body	Plant	Element
Ram	Aries	Head	Fruit	Fire
Bull	Taurus	Neck	Root	Earth
Twins	Gemini	Arms	Flower	Air
Crab	Cancer	Breast	Leaf	Water
Lion	Leo	Heart	Fruit	Fire
Virgin	Virgo	Bowels	Root	Earth
Scales	Libra	Reins	Flower	Air
Scorpion	Scorpio	Secrets	Leaf	Water
Archer	Sagittarus	Thighs	Fruit	Fire
Goat	Capricorn	Knees	Root	Earth
Waterman	Aquarius	Legs	Flower	Air
Fishes	Pisces	Feet	Leaf	Water

crops are planted in a water sign. There are many old sayings about planting by the signs, such as "plant corn in the heart", "don't plant potatoes in the feet", "dig potatoes in the new of the moon." Although I don't necessarily believe every bit of it, I don't necessarily disbelieve it either. I like to experiment with this old-time way of thinking by keeping track of when we plant and how the crop does, and I'm always interested in sign folklore.

Some almanacs offer a different view of planting by the signs. Aries, Gemini, Leo, Virgo, Sagittarius and Aquarius are the barren signs. When the moon is in them you cut weeds so they don't resprout. Leo is the best for cultivating. The fruitful, productive signs are Taurus, Cancer, Libra, Scorpio, Capricorn and Pisces. Cancer and Scorpio are regarded as number one and two for planting.

If you prepare a garden bed when the moon is in Capricorn, many weed seeds will sprout. In two weeks the moon will be in Leo, a barren sign, and a thorough cultivation will destroy all of the little weedlings. In a few more days the moon will be in the good planting signs of Libra and Scorpio and seeds sown now will get a good jump on the next crop of weeds.

A waxing moon is one that gets brighter every night, starting with a crescent moon in the western sky at sunset, and rising an hour later every night. Two weeks later, it rises as a full moon in the east just as the sun sets, and this is the traditional time to plant above-ground crops. A waning moon is the two-week period from full moon to new moon, which is the time to plant root crops and cut brush. The moon affects the earth's water, as demonstrated by higher tides along the ocean at full moon, and plants are full of water. Another cycle is the ascending and descending moon, which refers to whether the moon gets higher or lower in the sky each night. When the moon is in its lowest point in Sagittarius it starts to ascend, and its daily arc through the sky gets wider. This ascending moon phase is the time to harvest crops because the plant saps are rising also. Gemini is the zodiacal constellation highest in the sky and after the moon passes through it, the descending moon or planting time begins. When the moon is in the exact plane with the sun and earth, twice each month, then you should not work with plants at all, especially during eclipses.

Although we try to follow the moon and planets across the Zodiac and work with plants accordingly, the weather is a much more determining factor on what we do each day. After all, nature is forgiving, and if you plant in the wrong sign, a few days later the right sign will come along and it all works out. I used to scoff at planting by the signs as unscientific, but a broader view of nature reveals the interconnectedness of all things, and it is probably more unscientific to disregard anything.

July 15, 1997

Thanksgiving

> *"In the darkness of the earth the seeds are awakened,*
> *In the power of the air the leaves are quickened,*
> *In the light of the sun the fruits are ripened,*
> *Thus, in the shrine of the heart the soul is awakened,*
> *In the light of the world, the spirit is quickened,*
> *In the glory of God our powers are strengthened."*

This verse by Rudolf Steiner often comes to mind before I eat, comparing my life to a plant's life. A thankfulness runs through this blessing to the forces of earth, air and light that allow plants to flourish and consequently us humans who live from the giving of the plant world.

It implies a seed is in our hearts, a sacred place that grows and becomes our soul. As this soul is awakened, we become who we are and are grateful for our consciousness. The world then works on us, alternately building and destroying our spirit through our interactions with it and each other. These experiences also define our selves, and we try to be thankful, though it certainly is easier with some people and events than others.

We are thankful for the sources of our powers beyond our own selves and the small part we can play. I'm grateful to be a farmer and thankful for the opportunity to grow so much good food to sell and share.

So a big thank you to all the plants that make our life possible. A big thank you, too, to all the animals which eat plants we cannot and then provide us with food and fertilizer. And a huge thank you to the people in our community whose love and kindness shine through our interactions. I am especially grateful to be able to share my soul with yours.

Happy Thanksgiving.

November 25, 1997

Valerian

Valerianaceae Valeriana officianalis

CHAPTER VIII

A Tennessee Homestead

Root Cellar	207
Workdays	210
Greenhouse	212
Cold Frames	214
Solar Electricity	216
Outhouse	218
Patio	220
Wood	222
Farm Tour & Dinner	224
T.V. Show	226
Biodynamic Conference	228
Vision	230

"Begin it now. Until one is committed, there is hesitancy, the chance to draw back, always ineffectiveness. Concerning all acts of initiative (and creation), there is one elementary truth, the ignorance of which kills countless ideas and splendid plans; that the moment one definitely commits oneself, then Providence moves too. All sorts of things occur to help one that would never otherwise have occurred. A whole stream of events issues from the decision, raising in one's favor all manner of unforeseen incidents and meetings and material assistance, which no man could have dreamed would have come his way. Whatever you can do or dream you can, begin it. Boldness has genius, power and magic in it. Begin it now!"

Goethe

Root Cellar

The root cellar is at the end of a winding, stone stairway. A carved wooden face on the door greets you as you enter our own personal cave. Rows of mason jars filled with berries and vegetables line the shelves. Baskets of potatoes and turnips sit on the floor, and on a stone slab rest quite a few bottles of homemade wine. I was an eager 17-year old, not quite "work-brickle," when my brother John and I started cleaning out this old cellar site. Caney Wright, our predecessor, had dug a hole in the ground and covered it with logs, tin and dirt many years ago. Needless to say, it had fallen in and looked awful snaky. We cleared out everything down to solid slate shelves on the sides and back walls.

We'd never laid rock before, but it was high time to learn. Each rock had to sit comfortably on the ones below, preferably spanning a couple of them to tie it all together. A pick dug the hole a little deeper, and the stone walls slowly went up. All of the other projects involved in getting our homestead started put the cellar on the back burner, so it wasn't until four years later that we were finally ready to pour the roof. My friend Jerry helped frame up an arched roof for me, and I invited some friends over for a work party. Since it rained that morning, we partied and didn't work, but when I left for the watermelon patch and the rain let up, my friends started mixing concrete. Once you start pouring a concrete slab, you want to continue so that it forms one big chunk. We had half of an old pickle barrel that we'd been using for a bathtub, and it could hold a bag of cement plus five times as much sand and gravel that we had hauled up from the creek. We laid pretty creek rocks on the form and shoveled the concrete on top, about five inches thick. It didn't go far. So we mixed another batch, and another, and another.

Meanwhile, about half of the party stayed in the house, drinking homebrew, cooking dinner and strumming guitars. In any given crowd, there are folks who like to work and folks who like to play. Darkness fell, and we were a long way from putting the hoes away, so I got out the coal oil lamps. But raindrops cracked the chimneys, so I pulled the old Willis Jeep around, and we finished up by the headlights. Eighteen bags of cement and five tons of sand and gravel later, we finally had her covered. After a midnight dip in the creek, we were grateful for the dinner the kitchen crew had prepared. But Eric couldn't find his trowel. After a few weeks, I got brave enough to don a hard hat and take down the form. It was beautiful, with the creek rocks on the ceiling held in by the cement on top of them. The whole root cellar was stone, from the slate rock walls which turned into stone walls that rose up to the new arched rock ceiling. But what was this flat diamond-shaped rock in the ceiling? Eric's trowel is still up there, and I guess it will be for a long time.

Oak and sassafras slatted shelves only lasted five years each. Now we have cedar shelves in the root cellar. A cedar box holds the herbal and manure preparations we make for compost piles and field sprays, and baskets hold our winter's supply of potatoes. Arkansas Black apples have kept until the following May, as have Kennebec potatoes. Onions, squash and sweet potatoes don't keep well there because it is too moist. One year, we put endive in the cellar to sprout in the dark. Carrots, beets, turnips and Jerusalem artichokes all keep well in the damp cellar, and it has cooled many a jar of Jude's and April's (our cows) fresh, warm milk. It stays about 55 degrees all year long, which seems plenty cool in the summer and feels quite warm in the winter. It's a safe place to store the canned goods because, unlike our cabin, it never freezes.

Apples and potatoes are not supposed to be stored together, so we built another, easier root cellar, sort of accidentally. One dry summer we decided to put in a thousand-gallon cement septic tank for water storage. It leaked, and, of course, they wouldn't take it back. Doug and Richard busted a hole in the roof of the tank and hinged a door on it. Then we put a hole in the floor connected to a drainpipe, so any water that gets in will go out. It is a short root cellar, only four feet tall, but it serves well to keep either the potatoes or the apples into the next spring. Buried underground, it never freezes, and it was relatively quick and easy to turn a botched holding tank into a useful cellar.

Visitors have commented on how our stone root cellar takes them back to old European villages they've seen. It has a solid, old-time feel to it. There is nothing prettier than rows of bright red raspberries and

Chapter 8 A Tennessee Homestead 209

tomatoes, yellow jars of sweet corn, green beans and peas, purple pickled beets, salsa, butterbeans and black-eyed peas. It is our summer's garden safely tucked away to feed us through the winter.

October 8, 1996

Workdays

Group work days are an integral part of our farm operation. How do I get so much done? With a little help from my friends. We raise somewhere between 8,000 and 10,000 pounds of potatoes every year, that much or more winter squash and sweet potatoes, and 1,000 pounds of garlic, along with many bushels of tomatoes, melons and other vegetables and fruits. We sell them to health food stores and customers all over Tennessee, so there is a lot of planting, picking and packing to do around here.

One of our first work days saw 20 people milling about, digging potatoes with pitch forks, with much swimming, picnicking and spud-spearing. I was anything but prepared, and although we all had fun and got the job done, we weren't too efficient. A turning point came in `89 when we built our 16 foot by 40 foot, two-story vegetable storage barn. Several of my friends were carpenters by profession, and when nine of them came over one day, we were all astounded by what preparation, planning, good tools, good friends and strong coffee could accomplish. By 9:00 o'clock, the supports were up, and the generator and skill saws were humming. While Steve and Andy cut rafters, Joe, Bob and Fuzzy nailed on siding, and Jerry, Dan, Robert and Greg nailed down joists and the second-story floor. Somewhere in there, Steve found time to cut a stairway, and it was nailed down just in time to climb up and put on the rafters. The whole building was ready for tin by the end of the day.

Barn raisings were common years ago, as friends and family went to each others' farms to help erect a building or to do farm work. The Amish and Mennonites, in particular, still rely on group effort to get tedious jobs done. An Amish minister explained once why they harvest wheat the labor-intensive way. "Every farmer could own a combine and thresh their own wheat, but then we wouldn't all get together to help, and we'd sure miss Sarah's chicken and dumplings on this Saturday and Mary's pies next week," he said. The community bonding is more important to them than speeding up the work with machines. Dinner is an important part of a work day. It's fun to share food. When we dig potatoes, we like to have potato salad for starters, then hash browns, baked potatoes and potato soup for the main course, with potato pie for dessert (just kidding).

  Many of our jobs are relatively easy, just boring to do by ourselves. We'll have wonderful visits with friends sitting around cutting potatoes, cleaning garlic or shelling beans. Other jobs are a huge amount of work. Planting and harvesting field crops requires a crew. Again, friends come to the rescue, pitch in and help. We are indebted to them and could not do it without them. Sometimes people will hear about our farm or be directed here and will stay and work for room and board. We've made many new friends this way. It's good to have a straw boss for a job, someone who can boss people around and see that the whole thing is organized and running smoothly. He or she should be thrown in the creek at the end of the day, so they don't let it go to their head.

  A diversified farm needs people-energy to run smoothly without excess machinery. People need fresh farm food and good outdoor country work. Many "city slickers" really appreciate a good sweat and blisters, although I bet they're glad to get back home. By having all your tools, baskets and equipment together, and with a clear plan in your head, a work day can be a joyous, uplifting experience. We can swap labor with our neighbors or food with our friends, and accomplish jobs we wouldn't tackle alone.

July 18, 1995

Greenhouse

We're getting our greenhouse ready for plants this week. Although we built it to start our seedlings, we use it for everything but that now. In 1977, we bought a book on how to build a solar greenhouse attached to your home. Although I'm not a carpenter, I got a few 2x4's and was soon banging away. The idea is to go out about eight feet from the south wall of the house, start upwards towards the house with a 60 degree wall, and come off the house with a 30 degree pitch. Then you put a door in and cover the whole thing with fiberglass.

We began by digging a pit, so we could be partly underground. We made a slip-form rock wall for the foundation, and then put up the walls and roof, which is transparent on the southern half. The low winter sun shines in through it, but the upper half of the roof is insulated so the high summer sun doesn't. After following a few leads on fiberglass panels we ended up south of Gallatin at a huge factory with coverings for solar collectors that had been to California. They hadn't been packed correctly and were slightly damaged, so the buyers sent them back. But they were good enough for us and we bought a truckload. The panels turned yellow after 10 years, and the plastic greenhouse looked out of place on our rustic cabin, so we rebuilt it with a vertical south wall with glass windows in it.

Our first crop in the greenhouse was 2,000 tomato plants. They grew beautifully and were soon ready to sell. We loaded them on our '56 Chevy pickup truck and drove them to Nashville, where I spent the rest of the day fixing the truck so we could get back home. That fall we transplanted a few Swiss chard plants in the beds at the bottom of the greenhouse. All winter long we ate off of those plants, and then we knew why folks build greenhouses. A vent on the floor of our house lets cold air drop into the greenhouse and an upper window lets warm greenhouse air back in the house. Plants give off oxygen while using carbon dioxide, so they like our spent air and we like their oxygen-rich air.

When we rebuilt the greenhouse, we raised the beds up off the floor with a 2 1/2 foot tall brick wall. Now you can stand in a narrow pit walkway while you work the beds or harvest greens. This gives the cold air a place to settle so it's not right on the plants. We don't have supplemental heat in there, just what the sun gives us. We do have three 55 gallon, black water drums for thermal mass, so the warmed water radiates warmth back into the room at night. A few years ago Debby and Steve designed a blanket. On real cold nights, we unroll this insulating cover over the outside of the whole greenhouse and tuck it in.

The beds are filled with rich soil, compost and rock dusts. This spring they got a special treat. Two hens were getting broody, and we wanted to move them out of the coop to raise their chicks. So the empty greenhouse beds became the nursery for raising up baby chicks. They scratched up the soil, fertilized it, and got us up every day with their morning peeping.

An exotic cactus, an asparagus fern, a huge aloe, a large rosemary and a few other plants have graced the shelves for many years. In the fall, we go to the garden and dig up plants for the beds. The sun in the winter is too low to grow big plants from seeds, but the parsley, celery, kale, oriental vegetables, Swiss chard and a few marigolds from the garden create a lovely garden space in the greenhouse all winter long. Except for the marigolds, these are all frost-hardy plants that like cool weather and supply us with salads and greens until we can start harvesting outside again next spring.

Aphids and white lice are a problem sometimes, especially by spring, so we don't start our seedlings in there anymore, though ladybugs are helping to keep them under control. A greenhouse is a great place to take in a deep breath during a gloomy winter day, the bright green plants perking you up with some extra-fresh oxygen. It makes you feel kind of green.

September 10, 1996

Cold Frames

The cold frame is where the action starts. Mine has seen a lot of action lately, as it is just being constructed, but the real action will happen when I plant it. The middle of February is the time to sow broccoli and cabbage seed for late-March transplants.

I've built many cold frames over the years, from simple panes of glass leaning against the south side of the barn, to elaborate plastic hoop houses. The idea is to face south with as much protection from the north as possible, and to slope the windows at a 30 to 40 degree angle in order to catch the winter sun. I had a spot picked out by the barn, but it was too close to where I blindly back up with loads of hay; not a good place for a glass house.

It dawned on me that this cold frame will be perfect for over-wintering a few vegetables, especially if I can walk out the back door of the house and throw a blanket over it. So I remembered a sunny spot right out the kitchen door near where a tomato plant had survived when it frosted elsewhere. Only by living and observing do we find out where the little microclimates are on our farm, and I'd found a nice, warm one close by.

Unfortunately, it was right on top of the gas line to the house. I wanted to excavate 18 inches on the high side, and we found the line about a foot deep. After thinking on it for a day, I decided to move the line. Otherwise, I'd forget it's there and bust it with a digging fork some fine day in the future. I got a section of line and a couple of couplings, and a lesson on how to flare copper.

"Who's got some old windows?" I asked a few friends and ended up at Huddleston Hill admiring a huge stack of them sitting outside.

"Take them all," the owner said and when we did, I noticed a pile of old bricks. "Take those too, if you can use them." Another load of brick at the landfill decided the matter. This cold frame would be able to withstand the big bad wolf's huffing and puffing.

I'd never laid brick before, so I got Phil to help. Not that he had, either, it's just that he likes learning new things, too, and he can make good mud. Sand and gravel filled our three by 12 foot hole in the ground, about four inches deep, and one by one the bricks went up towards the string line. Rule #1: make sure your line is where you want it and doesn't slip, before you start laying brick. We saved the nicer bricks for above ground level and dutifully cleaned them up afterwards with an old file for a pointing stick and a wire brush.

Cedar won out over sassafras for the honor of the wood to use for framing on top of the brick. Steve ripped it at a 30 degree angle lengthwise on the table saw from some two-by-fours his neighbor had. I decided on the lower angle to give more room in the bed. It will be a right triangle and we need 40 inches (the window's length) on the hypotenuse side. A trigonometry book gave us the cosine of a 30 degree angle to find our height of 20 inches and width of 35 inches. "Numbers are our friends" is a saying I'm reminded of once again.

A drain and more sand and gravel went behind the brick wall, and then it was time to start filling the inside of the new cold frame. Eight inches of horse manure got packed down in the bottom. It heats up more than other manures and will add warmth underneath our plants. Then a mixture of sifted compost, sand and soil finished filling the bed to about ground level, with a little diatomaceous earth mixed in to repel snails. Small rows are drawn with our mortar-sore fingers, and the little round treasures are lightly buried, to burst forth in a few days as the new troops for this year's cabbage patch. I'll wait about a month before I start tomatoes and peppers, as they don't need to go outside until May. Other plants to start now will be celery and the onions.

A bench went above the new cold frame for setting the windows on and to keep someone from stumbling into the bed in the dark. The brickwork fits in nicely with the landscaping, and gives me the courage to think about rebuilding the chimney of the cabin. It also turned a one day job into a weeklong job, but with good lessons and a much more permanent structure than my previous cold frames. My next one will be for starting sweet potato slips, and I'm getting excited just thinking about it, though I hope it won't be brick. I believe a simple wooden box, facing south, will be sufficient.

In the fall I'll transplant kale, parsley, celery and Chinese cabbage into the cold frame and let them fill it up with their luscious green leaves. As the rest of the garden goes to sleep for the winter, there will still be plenty of action in this bed.

February 15, 2000

Solar Electricity

Our home had no electricity for the first eight years Debby and I lived here in Macon County. We got our light from coal oil lamps and candles. When we insulated our house, the kerosene fumes became noticeable, and we decided to be the first on our block to try this solar electricity that we had heard about. In 1981, my buddies Basil and Craig traded me a couple of solar panels, and we fastened one end to the positive side of a car battery and the other to the negative side. Then we hung a tail light from my old Dodge Dart in the kitchen and voila`! electric lights. I couldn't believe how easy it was.

As time rolled on, we learned more. The batteries needed a regulator, just like a car, to keep them from getting overcharged. We put in a fuse box and ran our house wires to it so everything would have a fuse. With 20 amp fuses, we feel quite safe that they will blow before an electrical fire could ever happen. Car batteries are made to stay charged, not go up and down all the time like in our solar-panel system. So we used marine batteries for a while, but now we have golf cart batteries, and they have lasted for five years. These deep cycle batteries are six volts. We have them hooked up in a series so the six batteries are like having three 12 volt batteries, and they store hundreds of amp hours.

The only care the system needs is to keep the batteries clean and full of water. We check them once a month. The six panels we now have put out about 18 amps an hour. If we get six hours of sunshine on them, we get (6x18) 108 amp hours on that day. The lights we have use 2.2 amps an hour, so we have plenty of power for lights. We also run a portable tape deck and a small fan. A few years ago, we put a 12 volt motor in an old Maytag washing machine, and that, too, runs off our solar system. It doesn't use any more power than what the panels collect while we do the laundry. We can tell this because after doing the wash on a sunny day, the batteries are still fully charged. A friend gave us an old refrigerator that runs on 12 volts. We hooked it up, but it took all the power we had to get it cold, so we don't use it. They make special refrigerators for 12 volt systems which are super-insulated and super-efficient, but they are super-expensive, too - over $1,000. Any appliance which produces heat, not just power, will use much more electricity.

You can buy photovoltaic (solar) cells for between $100 and $200 a panel. The ones we have now we bought in 1984 (three for $1,000) and 1989 (three for $600). The panels charge at about half-power on cloudy days. A photovoltaic cell looks like a leaf, but the veins are made of a thin silver wire embedded in silicon. On one side of the silicon is phosphorus with a negative valance of three. On the other side is boron with a positive valance of four. Positive valence refers to the number of free electrons an atom has in its outermost shell, while a negative valence is the number of missing electrons in its outer shell. When the sunshine hits the solar cell, it excites the extra electrons in the boron and they are attracted to the holes on the other side of the cell where the phosphorus is. When they try to get over there, they are caught on the silver wire and whisked down to the batteries where they are stored for use as electricity in our home.

Solar cells were invented in the 1800's, and there are panels putting out electricity after 100 years of use. The only reason I can think of that solar cells are not used more commonly is that the sun can't be metered.

We have friends with very typical households and all the modern appliances - TV's, refrigerators and shop tools– all of which are run off a bigger solar cell system. With enough panels, you can get an inverter and run 110 volts AC and have everything you'd ever want to plug in. Our friends are very happy with their independence from the energy corporations and feel the initial outlay will save them money (and the environment) in the long run since they have no monthly light bills.

Solar electricity is a good idea for many reasons besides economics. As we have used much of the world's known oil supply, future generations will have to find other energy sources. We might as well start now. The remaining oil could be used to help set up more permanent energy stations, solar or another alternative energy source. Solar electricity is here in several homes in Macon County and is used to charge fences on many farms. With a little bit of investigation and investment, it could be used to power a lot more, saving the user dollars and the earth its resources.

March 1, 1994

Outhouse

Our first outhouse was a typical dark little building about the size of a small closet. I think we even had a crescent moon on the door. Although this was pretty primitive for kids who had grown up with indoor plumbing, it sure beat taking a walk in the woods, especially when it was raining. We had been using a bucket and digging a hole once a week to bury the contents. Needless to say, this was not a pleasant job. So we set in to dig a big hole and make a long-drop john. We had experienced and heard about different outhouses, most notably one above a pig pen with eager grunts awaiting the gift. No, this was not for us.

The pit gradually got deeper, an interesting study in soil layers. The subsoil starts at about a foot and gets much harder at two feet deep. The color turns lighter, and the soil is almost pure clay the deeper you go. At about seven or eight feet, I was through with the pick and shovel and was thinking about the new building. Why does it need to be small and dark? I had some eight foot by three foot fiberglass panels, leftover from our greenhouse project, that let in a pretty purple light but were translucent, meaning they could not be seen through. Two of these made up the east wall to let the morning sun in. I left the other walls open at head level and put screen up. The whole building is big, light and airy. Many visitors comment on how nice and comfortable it is. It even has a porch.

In an attempt to fill it less quickly, we burn the paper. We use wood ashes from the cook stove as a "flush" to cover the odor. The privy sits in a lilac hedge near an herb and flower garden. Knowing the hole would eventually fill up, I built the building on cedar posts so I could skid it off the hole. After ten years, it was getting near the top, and it was time to dig another one. Now, the easiest digging would have been right under the outhouse, but this did not sound fun at all. I hired a backhoe to dig an eight foot hole a few feet away, and what had taken me a week took him about an hour. I pulled the building over the new hole and covered the old one with a few feet of earth.

Although some folks use "nightsoil" as a fertilizer on their crops, I have an aversion to this. My feeling is it should not be used on cropland, but that when sufficiently composted, it would be good to use on pastures. There is no doubt in my mind that human waste should be put back on the land. After this hole fills up I may dig up the first one, which will then be ten years old, and spread it on some marginal pasture land away from the house. Then I'll pull my privy back over the first hole and cover the other one.

I've seen and smelled several composting toilets and have not been impressed. Nothing I would want in my house. As water pollution and shortages become bigger problems, I imagine odorless composting privies will be developed. Still, I don't know that I'd want one in my house, either. It just doesn't seem like something to do inside the house. I guess that's why I have an outhouse.

January 10, 1995

Patio

It's like putting a giant jigsaw puzzle together, except we may not have all the pieces. This is how I would describe laying our slate rock patio. One advantage we have, though, is that we can break the puzzle pieces to try to make them fit. I have always thought that the flat, black rocks in our creeks were a valuable asset on our farm. We've pulled out many during the years and used them as stepping stones around the house.

Both of my brothers have taken a few truckloads to their places in North Carolina and used them beautifully around their small trout ponds. You'd better get them while you can because they wash downstream when it floods. Phil and I had spotted many during the summertime dips in the creek and finally felt caught up enough on the farmwork to spend a few days playing. I love working (playing) with rocks. There is a certain meditative quality about the two of us carefully moving big rocks from natural settings in a pretty creek bed onto the bank, into a truck, and eventually into an artistic design around the home. We move slowly, using our legs to lift, not our backs, and continually picture how the stones will fit together.

Over the years, we've developed rigid criteria for a good stone. It has to be smooth and flat on the top side and have a few straight edges. A batch of round rocks will never fit together tightly. The slate that is flaky is passed by, too. We're not sure, but I think it's years in the running water that makes the ones we prefer smooth and not so easily flaked. Anything too thin (easily broken) or too thick (too heavy) we leave, but we do go for nice, big "two people" rocks. Pointy ones and triangles are handy for filling in the puzzle. We gathered more stones than we needed, so we had lots of rocks to choose from. The extras will find themselves as stepping stones off towards the outhouse or root cellar.

A curved, as yet unbuilt, brick planter is envisioned in this patio, so we lay a few curved rocks where we think it will go. Nice big stones are laid where the most traffic will be, like around the back doorstop. Creek gravel has been put down already, and we rake and shovel it around, then set the stone down and wiggle it to try and get it so it doesn't rock. You don't want a rock that rocks. Often it takes several times of lifting it back up, putting more sand and gravel down, or raking some away, to get the stone to set right. We have no gutter on the house, so we are sloping the patio away from the foundation. There is a lot of putting our heads on the ground to see how it looks. We want the rocks to be the same height so there are not any toe-stubbers.

Sue came by and soon is wondering if this rock maybe fits over there. Laying rock is contagious. Sometimes we set several rocks down without laying them in, just to see how the puzzle will fit. Invariably, it all changes by the time we actually lay them, but it gives us good ideas on how they match up. Phil has a wonderful whistle that automatically comes out of him when the rock finally fits into place. We can take an hour to get one rock right, or place five of them in 10 minutes. When we get frustrated and can't find a rock to fit, we have two options - load the kids up and head for the creek to look for more stones, or get the hammer out.

Chipping a corner off a slate rock is tricky. They easily crack where you don't want them to. Unlike limestone, where a chisel works well, I've found just small taps with the hammer on the edge of the slate can sometimes make it fit. If it breaks in the wrong spot, well, you still get to go down to the creek. We don't resort to the hammer very much. It's much more aesthetically pleasing to find the natural rocks that fit together. Two days of playing has taken the 12 foot wide patio another 20 feet lengthwise along the house. It looks like it's been there for years already, just natural slate rocks with sand and gravel between them. Most of my playing is with plants which form an intricate jigsaw puzzle in the garden, but disappear with the seasons. This jigsaw puzzle is here to stay.

November 16, 1999

Wood

"Wood warms you twice: once when you cut it and again when you burn it." This old saying is quite an oversimplification, as it seems to me that wood warms you at least a dozen times. We often cut tops from logging operations nearby, but this year we have some trees down from last winter's ice storm. It's nice to hang out in the woods this time of year with all the bare branches reaching up towards the sky like nerve endings. The bluffs and hillsides stand out more, and you can picture all the life that a few months ago was teeming everywhere and is now resting within the earth awaiting spring.

Red oak is one of my favorite firewoods. Its straight grain makes it easy to split, and it isn't as stringy as white oak, though they both burn good and hot. The denser the wood is, the hotter the fire will be and the longer it will last. Hickory tops the list, followed closely by the oaks, hard maples, beech, walnut, cherry and ash. I don't mess with large elms - too hard to split - or the soft woods like poplar, willow and pine. We worked up some cherry yesterday, and it flew apart easily, with beautiful pink, orange and red grain. Beech and sugar maple tend to be more knotty and hence harder to bust. Walnut splits easily. It has a distinctive smell and a deep brown color.

Close attention to sharpening the chainsaw will make cutting a whole lot easier. I use a vise to keep the saw steady. "Safety first" is the rule with a chainsaw. Always be aware of what you are doing and where the tension is on the log. Don't be in a hurry. Enjoy the silence when you shut the saw off. Everything seems extra quiet and still then. Most likely your first layer of clothing will be off while you're cutting, and your sweater won't last long as you start splitting wood.

I used to use an old-fashioned maul and axe, with a sledge and wedge for the tougher stuff, but now I have a monster maul. The big triangular head is heavier and heats you up fast, often splitting the wood on the first whack. While it is the easiest to split, the ash I've been working on is over 18 inches in diameter and needs to be "daisied." This is where I split off pieces from the side rather than starting off right through the center like I usually do. As I walk around the log, the split sections fall off like the petals of a big daisy. My father showed me this when I was a kid, and also taught me to look in the center of the log for a small crack, and aim at that. By setting the logs upright the way they grew, they'll split more easily.

Now we have another warming job as we haul the wood to the pick-up truck. More heat is generated as we stack it on the truck, not throwing it on as we did last year when we broke out the back window of the truck. Back at the wood shed, we get yet another chance to warm up, throwing the wood off the truck, and then again while stacking it.

Old-timers have taught us to cut our wood a year in advance, as the dry wood burns so much better. The seasoned wood is stacked on a wheelbarrow and warms us as we haul it to the front porch, and then again as we bring it into the house. Other little warming jobs are cleaning the chimney, gathering kindling, and hauling the ashes back to the fields, where they are spread thinly, supplying valuable potash, calcium and trace elements.

The radiant heat of a wood stove seems to warm you differently than heat from a furnace. I wouldn't trade it for any other kind of heat, although the warmth we get from burning the wood seems minimal compared to the warmth we've generated getting it.

January 3, 1995

Farm Tour & Dinner

On Friday, July 26, about 80 people showed up at the Donoho Hotel, responding to our offer for an organic farm tour, lectures and dinner. Pam was in charge of registration, and most people paid the full $30.00 for the whole day. A few folks paid $15.00 for just the afternoon lecture and tour, and a few others came later for dinner. As if I wasn't nervous enough, Albert set up a video camera and taped my first lecture outside near the veranda. I started out emphasizing the importance of organic matter, then talked about compost and cover crops. The many questions helped keep things lively, and before I knew it the hour was gone and I'd only gotten through a quarter of my notes.

Steve carried about half of the participants down to the farm on a hay ride, and the others braved our driveway in their vehicles. Meanwhile, back at the hotel, the kitchen crew was already peelin' taters, washing vegetables, and cooking up a storm. Debby showed one group around the house, and after a demonstration of our old Amish fanning mill (for cleaning wheat), I took the other group up the hill. Again, their interest and questions kept things moving, and I talked about corn, pruning fruit trees and the vegetable varieties we grow.

We met back at the pond, where Albert explained the shiitake mushroom operation and how to grow them. Then we switched groups, and while I took the first group up the hill, Debby took my group down to the house and showed them the rock gardens, raised beds, herbs, flowers and the greenhouse. Then we all went down to the creek, where Chris and Christy served fresh melons and herb tea.

There were so many interesting people I wish we could have just visited for hours, but it was soon time to head back to the hotel. Sally and Phil were picking sweet corn and cabbages while we were touring the gardens, and back at the hotel, the owner was pulling his hair out. He had to feed his hotel guests and get that cleared up, along with another group to feed at 9:00, while about a half dozen helpers were in the kitchen scrambling to get our people served. At 6:30, the teenagers were bringing out the dinner, and what a beautiful sight it was. Jessy, Erica, April, Ina, Shanti, Renee, Ellie and Veronica carried out dishes of sweet corn, potatoes, pasta with mushrooms, casseroles, stuffed chard leaves, beef stew, cole slaw, beet borsch and homemade breads, all fresh from our farm and prepared that day. Herbal iced tea and spring water were poured, and laughter, chatter and chomping filled the Donoho dining room. Then out came the fresh blackberry, blueberry and apple pies, zucchini bread, whipped cream and cheese cakes.

The applause was deafening when we brought out the cooks and helpers: Jennifer, Lissa, Michele, Sally, Sharon, Katie, Linda, Jay, Jim, Paul and probably a few others. We shared a little homemade wine and then retired back outside to the veranda, where I attempted to explain biodynamic farming. We socialized afterward for a couple of hours, then I showed people where to camp, and we got home pretty late. But we were up again in a few hours, picking more vegetables to take downtown to the annual Red Boiling Springs Folk Medicine Festival to make lunch. We served close to 300 people - fresh salads, homemade bread and roasted sweet corn, again with the help of friends, strangers, and whoever would wash their hands and cut up with us.

All in all, it was a great celebration for everybody, although a little hectic in the kitchen. Many people said they had a great time, learned a lot and would love to do it again. A big thank you to everyone who helped make this weekend such a fun and rewarding time.

July 30, 1996

TV Show

It all started at the Folk Medicine Festival three years ago. I was making salads and selling vegetables with gusto and enthusiasm. Believing that healthy soils make healthy food and healthy people, I was excited about turning people on to fresh organic salads. Food is the best medicine, and I figured one of the reasons old folk remedies worked was because those people ate locally grown food from small sustainable farms.

I always meet a lot of people during the weekend of the "Weed Show", as Art Driver calls the festival, and, of course, everyone has a line or a story. So I didn't think much about it when a lady came back from getting her plate of vegetables and a Barefoot Farmer book to say, "I produce a TV show and we'd like to do one with you." Sure, I said to myself after she introduced herself as Carol Cornsilk.

Lo and behold, next spring we got a call and they came out to shoot the first Volunteer Gardener show. I have this personal grudge against TV and its will-destroying capabilities, so I insisted on actually making a two-ton compost pile. They were saying "just throw a few forkfuls for the camera" and I continued to unload a pickup full of manure and mix it with garden refuse, soil and leaves.

Many folks commented on how I got the host, Malcolm, to help with the shoveling, though he seemed to know when the camera was rolling and when it wasn't. They thought a minute-long demonstration of me stirring the biodynamic preparation would be sufficient, but again I insisted on stirring the full 20 minutes. I actually got a full day's work in during the filming, with Carol and Keith the cameraman sort of chasing me around.

I thought Malcolm did a great job of explaining the biodynamic approach of looking at the forces involved in agriculture rather than just the substances. It is not an easy concept to grasp, let alone discuss on TV. I do wish they had cut the scene out with me scratching my crotch, but I guess I was just acting naturally and it did make my friends laugh.

Our second program was on seed saving and the fall garden, and my favorite shot was digging those sweet potatoes. I hadn't dug any yet, so we were all genuinely surprised when the first hill popped up so many perfect sweet potatoes. The fall garden looked superb in that show, with the dark green Bok choy running away with the Oscar Award. Our dog got a runner up award for best actor.

This year, Carol wanted short, five-minute segments on organic gardening tips. Of course I had to start out with soils, cover crops and compost, all of which she thought would be too boring. But I can't talk about organic vegetables without bringing up compost for bringing in life forces, cover crops for building soil structure and basic good soil husbandry. She relented, and I suppose the first three shows are a bit boring. We've filmed 22 altogether.

Not owning a TV, I haven't seen most of them yet, but many people have. They are on Nashville Public Television, Channel 8 at 7:30 Thursday evenings every other week and on Sunday morning at 9:30. It's not like I have a script or anything; I just kind of rap about the subject. I talk about gardening all the time, so it comes easy, until they put a camera in my face. All of a sudden there is not a lot to say or think. "This is a squash plant, duh. That is a watermelon, duh".

The heat was rough on the crew, and of course, our gardens are in full sun. After finishing the spring garden segment on onions, peas, beets, carrots, parsley and lettuce, I wanted to show them the acre and a half potato field. It's a great example of how soils affect plant growth and insect populations. On the lower, richer part of the field, the plants are bug-free and knee high, with beautiful foliage and growth. The upper side of the field has poorer soil and the plants are stunted and have Colorado potato beetles infesting them, a prime example of the importance of building good soils. But the crew was burnt out and headed for air-conditioned Nashville instead, so if y'all want to check it out it's the field on the left in the curve right before the Heady Ridge bridge.

It was only about 6:00 and I hadn't done much physical work all day. So I hiked up to the mulberry trees and picked until "little dark". When I got back to the house, I was surprised to find Dustin Hoffman had left a message for me with plane fare to Hollywood.

June 15, 1999

Biodynamic Conference

The biodynamic preparations were the main theme at our gardening conference this year. Ninety adults registered, so we were feeding over 100 folks if you count kids and staff. Hugh Lovel summed it up in his keynote address on Friday night entitled, "Biodynamics in a Nutshell." He said, "Biodynamics is simply the best eating."

We had just finished homemade chili, buttered butternut squash, Chinese cabbage salad, baked potatoes and fried apple crisp, so we couldn't help but agree. Everything this weekend, as at all our events, was homegrown biodynamic food: wheels of cheese, butter, milk, cream, meat, tomatoes, greens, potatoes, apples, squash, sweet potatoes, peppers, peaches, pears, wine, garlic, basil, onions, pinto beans, watermelons, corn and wheat for the 50 loaves of bread. Participants were shelling beans, harvesting and chopping veggies, and grinding corn throughout the weekend.

After Christy's raspberry jam disappeared at breakfast Saturday morning, Bob Luzader led off with an explanation of homeopathy. Biodynamics is sometimes referred to as homeopathy for the land because we use potentized preparations. Bob has studied it for many years and had everybody potentizing homeopathic remedies. Meanwhile, back at the barn, Hugh Courtney spent all morning going indepth about the biodynamic preparations like only he can do. Everyone got a chance to stir all nine of them and spread them on the garden and fields. Cow horns were stuffed with manure and buried, and the compost pile was prepped. By noon, Hugh was hoarse, and newcomers to biodynamics were quite wide-eyed. I showed off the Shiitake mushroom operation and we harvested them for dinner.

At 10:00, Hugh Lovel began a workshop on energy, but 11:00 soon rolled around and Harvey Lisle gave an inspiring sermon on the practical aspects of spiritual farming. Many of the lecturers stressed that we are all more powerful than is commonly believed and that we can work with Mother Nature to heal the earth. Lunch and free-time followed, then Charles came by with the hayride for a tour of the farm. We wandered through rock gardens full of fall vegetables, flowers and herbs, and up the hill to a corn patch. Here we looked at the fibrous roots and learned how hay crops, compost and cattle create this farm organism. Further up the hill, we ate pears in the orchard and then saw a demonstration of a double-digging spading machine.

Back at the conference center, we introduced ourselves in a circle and expressed our hope and love for the people who show care for the land. From doctors and lawyers to farmers and gardeners, from folks in their 80's to little babies, it was an enthusiastic crowd supporting good farming practices in the Southeast. After a delicious dinner topped off with the butternut pies we had made early Saturday morning, we had our fund-raising auction where people brought stuff they had made or grown and everyone got a chance to bid. A bonfire enticed a dulcimer outside, while in the dining room guitars and folk songs filled the air.

Sunday morning found us reading chapter four of Rudolf Steiner's Agriculture Course, with Lovel, Courtney, myself and others offering commentary. It's great to have people with years of biodynamic experience nearby when you try to understand concepts like astral and etheric forces. The rest of the day was spent in informal clusters with the speakers.

Lunch was our last meal together, so afterwards we again gathered in a circle and sang a song. Harvey suggested we spend a moment in silence to meditate on healing the earth. It was powerful, and we all took home a newly inspired hope. A big round of applause was given to the cooks, the lecturers, the food, the weather and the wonderful children. An even bigger thank you goes out to the Biodynamic Association whose gracious funding helped support this conference, to the Tennessee Alternative Growers Association who organized it and to the people who came to learn and to share.

September 28, 1999

Vision

I can't say as I've done much farming during the snowy days, except for feeding the cows, but I have been busy at another favorite occupation of mine - coming up with ideas and visions. As I like to write about what I've done each week, this week I'll try to share some of my visions. Red Boiling Springs used to be a health resort and could be again.

The first is a health food store at the local fruit market. Have you ever seen those huge walk-in coolers? There is enough room for five semi-truckloads of produce in them. We could store all of Macon County's potatoes throughout the winter. Local farmers could bring in fresh vegetables all summer and cool them off right away. A delivery system could be set up to truck them to customers all over the area. In the fall, we'd fill it up with potatoes, sweet potatoes, cabbages, carrots, beets and other storage crops to insure that we would have plenty of good food over the winter. The store could stock dried beans, corn meal, winter squash and and other homegrown vegetables, along with local herbs and fruit.

As the health food business continues to boom, Red Boiling Springs would be the place to go for good food. Along with this, we could set up canneries and other food processing plants. The number two vegetables would be made into salsa, pickles and jams, and frozen, dried and otherwise preserved. For example, I heard of a potato chip factory which was started with a $30,000 investment in machinery. Marketed now throughout Louisiana, it's keeping local farmers busy raising potatoes. A value-added product is a locally produced farm product that is processed further into a marketable item. We can keep small farmers busy raising food crops, have locally owned processing plants, and sell ready-to-eat products, keeping the jobs and money flowing around here.

A bakery could be supplying our breads and other baked goods, made fresh every morning by someone who likes to get up early. Maybe combine this with a coffee and donut shop or a health food restaurant. A micro-brewery would be the place to go on Saturday nights for a dark, frothy homebrew. Local musicians could get the crowd dancing and singing along. A slaughterhouse could be packing all our cows, pigs and chickens for meat products, rather than us selling the animals at market prices. I don't guess hamburgers are half-price even though cattle are.

The local dairies would put out delicious ice cream, with fresh blackberries in July. Milk, cheese and butter could all come from Macon County pastures, without bovine growth hormones, please. Free range chickens could supply us with much better eggs than those caged-up birds in modern factory-farm chicken houses. Food is the most valuable of all products, and we can grow most of it here. When we buy cheap food products shipped in from elsewhere, we are supporting an agricultural system that may or may not be sustainable and healthy.

An electrical co-op could be set up to start generating solar electricity. New homes could incorporate passive solar heating and environmentally friendly products. Instead of exporting logs and pallets, we could mill a much smaller fraction of our timber each year and export only finished wood products.

One of the great resources of Macon County is its natural beauty and clean water. Parks could be developed with nature trails to cliffs, waterfalls and caves. People would come just to see clear creeks, wildlife and big trees, if we can save them. Herbs, homeopathy, acupressure and many other health care alternatives are effective, and coupled with good food, rest and the strength of our wilderness areas, we could make this area a true healing center. Again, we grow the herbs, make the medicines and learn the arts of healing ourselves.

A local school could bring in college kids who want to learn practical skills in organic food production, fine woodworking and alternative healing. We'd get paid to teach them, and they'd get college credits. We need a place for younger kids to go to learn more about nature, a museum with skeletons of all the local wildlife, a trail with identified, local plants and trees, and a school with a holistic approach to learning that lets a child's lifetime-calling mature and become real. Being proud of our heritage, we could also rescue and teach the old crafts of our early settlers here. Tanning, soap making, wood-working, quilting, weaving, pottery and many other homesteading chores produce valuable products and hone skills.

  Setting up local businesses like these would also call for bookkeepers, accountants, promotional people, sales representatives and many other jobs. Instead of selling our county and town to the highest bidder, I believe we have a real choice now to create a sustainable, healthy, safe place to live and raise children. By taking care of our own needs and preserving the natural beauty of our forest and wilderness, a strong, healthy community could be built that would offer some solutions for the future.

January 16, 1996

Lettuce carrot to the beet of peas
I've bean corny so long
I squashed the tomatoes and peppered the potatoes
Bean out in the garden too long

An organic grown is coming from a watermelon
See what my honeydew
She parsleys with a parsnip and turns into a turnip
I never know what she's into

There's eyes and ears and heads in these beds
Don't radish the celery
I got plum peachy with a pear of boysenberries
And brussel sprouted the broccoli